EDD WIL

G000122494

IS YOUR SCHOOL
LYING
TO YOU?

GET THE CAREER YOU WANT
GET THE LIFE YOU DESERVE

Ortus

First published in 2017 by
Ortus Press
An Imprint of
Free Association Books

A CIP Catalogue of this book is available from
the British Library

ISBN: 978-19113831-2-3

Cover design and typeset by
www.chandlerbookdesign.co.uk

Printed in Great Britain by
4 Edge Limited

To my wife and children who made me
start taking the future seriously and
indulged my efforts. Thank you.

CONTENTS

INTRODUCTION

'To travel hopefully is a better
thing than to arrive.'

Robert Louis Stevenson

The guy who wrote the above quote is dead. He went on to say, 'and the true success is to labour'. That is to say, hard work is its own reward. Only that's not really true, is it? Ask anyone working back-to-back shifts in a warehouse for minimum wage how fulfilled they feel and you'll likely get a stony stare in response. It's honest work for sure but dollars to doughnuts the people doing it are probably wishing they could do something else. Hope is good, but hope doesn't open doors, or get you the life you want; it's like my Grandpa always said, 'Hope in one hand, poop in the other - see which gets full first.'

I was lucky enough to get a scholarship to go to a private school. It was fairly liberal and progressive and was generally regarded as pretty good; but they cheated me. I don't tell you this to look in any way special, quite the opposite - it's to highlight the fact that this is a universal problem. Every school, every student no matter what their background, is likely going to be let down through a combination of bad advice and stupid advice. Unfortunately for you, your school is fixing to do the same to you. They won't mean to of course but if they haven't already, they are about to start. Mine didn't do it through malice, just ignorance - the guy responsible for careers and university admissions had been cloistered in a grace and favour house on the school grounds for nearly three decades. That is to say, his most recent experience of any of the stuff he was charged with teaching was his own exposure to it after finishing his degree. To clarify, a man who last interviewed for a job twenty-five years ago was telling us how the job market works. He would use phrases like, 'in the real world' as if that had some meaning for him. You wouldn't opt for surgery from a keen amateur who had watched Casualty twenty years ago, but this was pretty much the same thing - we were putting our lives in the hands of a man who was thoroughly unqualified to do the job.

Does this sound familiar to you? Somewhere in your building is a very nice, well meaning person who has lots of books about the types of jobs there are, lots of leaflets, some box-ticking psychometric forms with leading questions like, 'are you interested in pursuing a career in the law?' They probably used to work for Connexions, a careers service paid for by the government that has since been disbanded. The vast majority of these people are lovely and sincere people who have spent years building a network of local businesses that are well disposed enough to them to allow a gaggle of students to do some work experience or to come in and do a speech on careers day about an exciting life in the plastics industry. The trouble is if they've spent their working life doing that they don't really have any concept of what an employer is actually looking for, or how to interview. Or how to get the best internships, how to network, how to write a CV or a personal statement. In fact, of all the practical skills you'll need to acquire there's not much they can offer beyond the broad strokes. You may leap to defend them of course and dismiss me as being a 'big ol' meany' but these are, I'm afraid, the facts. Ofsted says so, the Department of Education says so, the Sutton Trust says so, the Local Education Authorities say so, employers are saying so. In fact the only people who aren't saying so are the schools. Makes you think - who has most to lose?

So, set against the rather depressing backdrop of these facts, what can you do? In this book I'm going to set out in plain terms what you can do, when you should be doing it and how to do that thing you should be doing. For those of you lucky enough to know what it is you want to do with or get from your life then, assuming you're willing to do some of the hard yards, this should be plain sailing. For those of you who are still uncertain, it's less clear, but avoiding making a decision is in many ways making a decision anyway, so I'm going to set out some best practice activities and techniques that are universally applicable whilst you start to identify possible pathways, and again it should all be cream cheese.

There are a mix of practical exercises, hints, tips and how-tos that cover all the aspects I believe are necessary to best position yourself for your life and career post-school, whether that takes you into an apprenticeship, higher education or a year out doing something new and challenging. There are also a number of interviews with interesting people who have led interesting lives doing interesting things with their careers. I have purposely not drawn any conclusions on what they have to say; I want you to take from their experiences that which is relevant to you. Some of it may even directly contradict some of what I'm telling you to do in the book, but whilst best practice and rule breaking make for odd bedfellows it goes back to what will become a familiar motto, there's no one right way but there are a lot of wrong ways. Sometimes following the steps I've suggested will create opportunities that will illuminate a more direct path to your goal, rendering other parts of the programme unnecessary, but this is not a happy accident; by following these guidelines you will proactively create opportunities for yourself and you will always be further ahead of the curve than you will be by doing the bare minimum suggested by your school.

At this point one would traditionally summon up a big finish designed to make you fist-pump the air and shout something. I don't have that, but more of a meek promise: I've been doing this for a while and if you do what I suggest then everything is going to be just fine. You hear that? Everything's going to work out. Phew, that's a load off, right?

1

THE HOWS AND WHYS OF DECISION-MAKING

'Life is what happens to you while you're busy making other plans.'

John Lennon

Self-evidently everything in life is a choice. Even the things that don't appear to be choices have choices attached to them, and how you react to them and the paths you choose have ripple effects with sometimes fleeting, but often lasting, consequences. For instance, from the moment your alarm goes off in the morning, you make a choice, do I hit snooze? Do I get up? If I hit snooze, will I have time to shower/eat breakfast, make it to school or college on time? If I choose to skip breakfast maybe I'll be hungry and because I'm focused on that I don't pay attention to something important in class. Maybe that's the thing that the entire exam is on and I miss out going to my first choice university because I dropped a grade. Then I end up getting a job I don't want to do and do it for forty years...

Obviously that's a slightly extreme example but it does illustrate the point pretty well: every choice you make has a consequence, sometimes tiny, sometimes big, but even lots of tiny, seemingly inconsequential consequences can, over time, create a real and genuine shift. This chapter is focused on highlighting the importance of the choices you make and underlining why and how you should make them.

Ask any adult if they feel any different now to when they were eighteen and the likely answer is that they aren't quite sure who the old person staring back at them in the mirror is. As a teenager there are lots of scientific reasons why you process time differently to adults, and conceptual thinking is something acquired through experience rather than being innate, so seeing the present as an irritating preamble before your real life begins is very easy and entirely understandable; it is not, however, useful to you.

What you do now, the decisions you make right now, regardless of how old you are or where your ambitions may take you, have an impact. By ignoring the present and not making choices you are in fact making a choice. Letting life wash over you without ever making a conscious decision is making the choice to settle for whatever turns up - which isn't necessarily ideal.

Unfortunately for you, little brain worms are constantly munching at the decision-making portion of your mind, making any choices a lot harder than a simple yes or no, and lots of internal and external biases are subtly influencing your decisions. That is to say, if you believe your decisions are logical, you're probably not paying proper attention. Hidden tendencies or preferences distort the decision-making process without us even knowing.

Example: Who shot JFK?

Since Kennedy's assassination in 1963 a veritable cottage industry has grown up dedicated to solving the mystery of his death. Films, TV dramas, documentaries and in the last fifty years or so more than 2,000 books are all desperately trying to persuade us that theirs is the correct account. Each establishes an argument and then presents the evidence to support its case. Or, rather, they all begin with a theory and conclusion and then root out the evidence to support that conclusion.

This is what is known as confirmation bias and it shows a jaw-dropping fissure in how we approach complex questions. Many of our decisions are based not on the material facts, but on the application of our hidden leanings and reasoning that we justify in support of that leaning. That is to say, we approach most decisions with a view and then fill in the blanks to support our decision.

Why is this relevant to you? If your decision to go to university is based on the supposition that that is just what you're supposed to do because of your parents or societal pressure, you will find the arguments to support that decision regardless of whether it makes sense for the career you want to pursue. If you want to work in the leisure industry or in tourism and hospitality, doing a degree in the subject is, in all probability, much less useful than working in the summer as a tour rep, interning and getting experience. Equally, if you come from a background where you make the assumption that university is for 'other people' because your parents and people in your circle haven't gone, you are unfairly limiting your potential based on how you perceive yourself, a perception that is informed by other people's opinions. Not facts. Opinions. But opinion can very quickly become fact if you don't examine it closely.

In his book, *Thinking Fast And Slow*, the Nobel Prize-winning behavioural psychologist Professor Daniel Kahneman illustrates our two types of thinking - the first is rational, logical, analytical and unhurried; we know it's happening as it happens, such as in an exam when you're 'actively' trying to solve a problem or answer a question. The other is fast, instinctive, intuitive and happens instantaneously without premeditation or forethought; it's you on autopilot. Often the poor choices we make and the biases that drive them are a result of our 'trusting our gut' rather than making an informed, logical choice.

Here's a famous example, which is likely apocryphal, but as an idea it works. Doctors in a study were asked to choose between two types of medicine for 600 people suffering from a fatal disease. Treatment A, which was positively framed as 'saving 200 lives', was dramatically favoured over treatment B, which was negatively framed as 'leaving 400 to die'. If you were paying attention it's obvious that both treatments generated exactly the same result. It's simply that A leads with the good news.

'Heuristics' is the name for the shortcuts we take when we need to make a decision quickly: relying on an innate sense, often based on experience, that certain things just work in certain situations. In essence an often imperfect but usually sufficient solution to a problem. Behind many of our everyday decisions is a subconscious mental arithmetic weighing whether you get the doughnut now or ten doughnuts in an hour's time. Short term gain almost always outweighs longer term gain. It's one of the reasons you leave your homework/ coursework/revision until the last minute in favour of playing *Call of Duty* or hanging out with your mates.

Even when we understand in our rational brain what delaying doing stuff means, we still readily write off the future; procrastination - 'understanding' the options and then choosing not to do what you ought to do - puts the burden on to tomorrow. Basically it would be like me saying, 'Don't sweat it, Future Edd will take care of that,' by which point, the chances are, whatever you are putting off will seem even bigger and more overwhelming.

Because we are all human and by nature irrational, we can never really be free of our biases but we can learn how to identify them as such. Rather than simply accepting the first thought or instinct you have to commit to a course of action or resolve an issue, you'd be better off taking a deep breath, being really honest with yourself and actively seeking out evidence against those assumptions and whether that 'gut' feel is loaded with bias.

Average everyday folk do not make wholly rational decisions. When problems are framed in terms of emotional gains and losses, our image of probability becomes **distorted** through the lens of loss aversion - that is, simply put, not wanting to lose out. The distortion is, however, predictable. Prospect theory understands the distortion and can allow us to predict when the sub-optimal decision-making will occur, something which I see all the time in my day job.

FOMO - Fear of Missing Out - this is a thing I hear the young folk talk about, right? It's actually a very real and persuasive influencer. Many of the choices we make accept as fact that an unlikely proposition may be true, even as we acknowledge the likelihood that the real outcome is unlikely to be as dramatic as the potential outcome, we worry that missing out would be worse than that disappointment. In essence we prioritise the potential loss over the likelier gain. We don't like to lose out. To put it in simpler terms, if I told you that there was a party at a friend's house, a pretty low key affair, a few mates, a BBQ and a sleepover - not a wild night but probably good fun and entirely bankable - but the other option was going to stand outside Tesco in Northwich, Cheshire in the rain because Harry Styles and Taylor Swift had been spotted there once, it would seem like an obvious choice to go to the party at a friend's house - to me at least as I have no interest in seeing either of them. However, to many people, as unlikely a prospect as it might seem, the fear of missing out would weight the decision towards standing outside the supermarket.

All of us are prone to these decision-making heuristics because humans are naturally loss averse. We fear loss more than we desire gains. Something tangibly bad or at least just okay seems better than an abstract good - knowing all that should make decision-making a little easier. That is to say, once you get that your brain can't necessarily be trusted, you're going to question it more.

Now, I know a lot of that information may seem a little bit scientific and mind-bendy but it's a very important thing to understand. If you can figure out *how* and *why* you make decisions, not only should they be easier to make, it should be easier to make the *right* decisions. I can't tell you what you should do with your life but I can urge you to really examine the motivations behind the choices you make regarding your academic and career plans.

A lot of students mentally write off huge swathes of options without a second thought - so here's a quick example for you: studying overseas. The vast and overwhelming majority of students in this country don't even consider it; it's not even a choice that comes into their head. Why not? Perception of cost perhaps, homesickness, they will miss their friends, family. All of these are valid but when you examine them closer you can see where the false assumptions come into play.

PERCEPTION OF COST - We all know for sure that US universities are far too expensive to even consider, right? Wrong. Yes, they are expensive but frankly many are on a par with UK universities now, plus there are a wealth of scholarships and bursaries available, and many operate on a 'needs blind basis' - that is to say, if they like you they'll pay for what you can't.

HOMESICKNESS - News flash: as you grow up you will have to move out. There's no way of knowing how you will feel about that until you do it. Putting an obstacle in the way or making a decision based on the perception of how you might feel just doesn't make sense. Fear of the unknown is natural but if approached sensibly it's a calculated risk.

YOU'LL MISS YOUR FRIENDS - Your friends will be off doing their own thing as well. You can't live your life for others and you can't go home again, as Thomas Wolfe so famously said; that is to say, things change. All the things that make your home your home are the people you surround yourself with, but those people will move on to the next phase of their lives and unless you want to be left behind you should too. I guess the point is you'll miss your friends no matter what, because things do change and so do your relationships: if you're lucky, for the better, but you don't want to be the one who never grew up.

FAMILY - No matter where you go or what you do, your family will miss you and they will worry, but fundamentally one would hope they want the best for you and if that means studying overseas they will understand and use it as an excuse to come for a holiday.

This one very small example highlights how an entire set of options is eradicated in one deft blow but not perhaps for any good reason, just an assumption that you're likely to study in the UK. If you want to get the career you want and the life you deserve you need to start taking those decisions seriously. You should go to the best possible place to do what you want to do, not the best place near to your home.

When you approach any of the decisions you'll be forced to make in the near and further future don't be afraid to think as big as you can. Why limit your options at this stage? Throughout your life you will be forced to compromise on any number of things but now, right now, the only person you need to consider is you. This is your life and you need to make sensible choices that will actively benefit your future. So dream big, the bigger the better - your reach should always exceed your grasp and don't be afraid to fail or be told no; it doesn't mean the decision was wrong, it just means you need to find a different route to pursue the same goal.

CASE STUDY
Oliver Jones, LLB, LLM

Oliver Jones is a practising barrister at 4 Paper Buildings, the UK's largest chambers of family law barristers. He is also a part-time Judge (Recorder since 2015). His practice is concentrated on Family Law dealing with all areas of public law and private law relating to children. His cases involve disputes between parents in relation to their children and also care proceedings (when social services intervene in a family to protect the children). He has experience in complex non-accidental injury cases, domestic violence, sexual abuse, neglect, terrorism and child abduction matters. He has been published in Family Law Week, the New Law Journal and has contributed to the Legal Network Television training videos.

ME: From way back in childhood did you always harbour ambitions of law and were the academic choices you made in support of that or was it more of a happy accident?

OJ: Not initially.,Iinitially I wanted to be David Attenborough. Then I wanted to be Richard Branson, and then somewhere along the line of the Richard Branson thing I thought to be a business-man it would be good to do law and that will tee me up for a successful business career. Then when I was about sixteen I did some work experience in family law. It happened that a person my father knew was one of the family partners in a solicitors firm in Covent Garden so I went along to that, thinking, 'Oh family law, it's parasitic nonsense, taking advantage of the misery of others.' But when I actually saw it in practice I realised that is not how it really feels when you're doing it. It's much more dealing with people who are in a terrible mess anyway and helping them find a way out of it. I thought that's quite interesting, it's got quite a human dimension. At that point, the megalomaniac business ambitions of my early teens had subsided anyway and I was more cued up towards a professional life and I thought that was quite interesting. So it was probably really from about sixteen that I thought I'd do law. So I picked A levels that would point me in that sort of direction - although actually you can do anything for law - and then I did a law degree. Which obviously helped...

ME: You said you can do anything for law. Given the challenges faced by young people trying to get pupillages now, with the Legal Aid bill being cut and so on, is there a particular background that you think would be favoured? Are there certain subjects that more easily make sense to someone reading a CV?

OJ: No. Basically no, not really. You need to get a 2:1; in theory you could become a barrister with a 2:2 but in practice that's rarer than hen's teeth, so you need to get a 2:1, and the more established, better regarded universities tend to produce candidates that dominate the field. It's not necessarily a bar if you are at one of the less renowned universities; it's just that it's harder. But that's not just because of the degree; it's because of the A levels and everything else. In terms of whether you have to do a law degree, that's absolutely not necessary. A lot of people do another degree and then do a one year conversion course. If you do a degree in law then obviously you're getting quite an in-depth education in the way that law is understood, cases are analysed and things like that. Whereas if you do a conversion course, they condense it down to the bare bones over the course of a year and it becomes much more about the practical basis, getting the basic knowledge but without working through the jurisprudence of it. I don't know whether doing a law degree makes you a better lawyer or not. On the other hand there's the school of thought that says going off and doing French, English, History, Science or Maths or whatever else makes you a more rounded person: maybe that's better.

ME: So what did you actually do for your undergraduate degree?

OJ: I did law at UCL as an undergraduate. Then I did Bar School.

ME: And then you went and did your LLM?

OJ: Yes, I went on to get my Masters of Law. After that I did a pupillage for one year. After twelve months of pupillage you are able to practise but you have to secure a tenancy within chambers to work from. That can take more time still and lots of people have to do further pupillages, or 'third sixes' with another set of chambers before they can secure a tenancy.

ME: It's obviously very hard now to break into this world. Was it hard then too? Have you seen a change?

OJ: It was massively competitive, really hard - even then. I think it is getting harder still now. There are less pupillages available than in my day and the numbers applying remain very high.

ME: So what do you think gave you the edge? Did you have a lot of work experience? Did you have connections? What did you do to give yourself the best chance?

OJ: First time I went round I didn't get pupillage, I got lots of near miss offers. I had reserve offers for a few places but they didn't come through. I got a decent number of interviews but I hadn't got on. I think I did all those applications when I was about twenty-one years old and my lack of experience in life generally showed. A lot of people do something else after university and then go across to the Bar and I think the greater confidence you have, from experiencing something other than just education, probably helps. Sometimes I see candidates who have come straight from university looking a little bit more nervous and finding it a bit harder. So in my case I got a year older and did my Masters and then I went round again and secured my pupillage and off I went. But in terms of what people do nowadays, when I see a CV coming in I see people are doing mooting, debating, they're involved in various activities, they do volunteering work, they go off and do death row work, or go to the Caribbean or the States or they do work on domestic violence in Eastern Europe or the former Soviet Union and all this kind of stuff and they do the most amazing additional things on top to the point where it has almost become the norm for the candidates we see, which is astonishing and almost kind of ridiculous really. But that's where it seems to be going. They're not the reasons we pick people in the final analysis though.

ME: Does it help in terms of getting an interview, do you think?

OJ: Maybe, yes. When we're working out our interview process we're looking at a series of criteria that we try to assess objectively and then we can compare fairly all the candidates. So academic achievement is one aspect of it, although we don't distinguish between universities in that. I don't know if other chambers do. Legal knowledge is another aspect of it but ultimately we're looking for a bit of an X factor about people, which is hard but you know it when you see it, whether that's charisma, intellect, eloquence, determination, ambition or a combination of those. Generally speaking most of the candidates are good lawyers, they can analyse, they can write and it becomes quite hard to distinguish but we tend to spot it when we see it. But of course then we take successful candidates for pupillage and we don't have to make a final decision for nearly twelve months which is a massive amount of time to get to know them and see how they develop. As a chambers we invest heavily in our pupils. We pay them quite generously during their twelve months and their pupil supervisors and other members of chambers spend a very long time training them. So we don't want to be getting it wrong. I think one of the key factors for getting through is tenacity; a lot of people get disheartened, give up and then don't become barristers whereas other people keep plugging away and then they do.

ME: You are now a Recorder (one of the types of judiciary - broadly equivalent to a circuit judge, having to sit a minimum of thirty days a year). Was that something you had always aspired to?

Would you describe your career as being the result of a very carefully thought-through plan or have you created opportunity for yourself and then it's taken you to places where you didn't necessarily think it was going to go?

OJ: It's a bit of a mix. I always had an enduring interest in family law. I did a mix of areas, when I first came to the bar, of civil, personal injury, criminal and family law, occasional other things, a bit of contract, a bit of immigration as well, a bit of employment but over time I narrowed it down and family was dominating my practice and then about eight or nine years ago I moved across to one of the leading children's law barristers chambers in the country and all the other areas of practice stopped. I've always harboured judicial ambitions and I was keeping an eye out in the last few years before I made my application. I was doing extra-curricular things outside of my work life with half an eye on making an application. So I was doing things like being a school governor and being involved in the community and I became a committee member for the bar standards board and things like that, knowing that that would be something that would augment an application. It wasn't entirely calculating - I had other reasons for being a school governor, in so much as the school was in trouble and my kids went to it so I wanted to help be part of the solution - those sort of things did help though and when they opened up the competition I went for it and I was lucky enough to get through.

ME: What's the next stage for you?

OJ: Well, I've got two types of career progression now, one is that I carry on at the Bar and maybe apply to become silk (that is another term for becoming a QC) and the other is to try and become a full time member of the judiciary and again I'd have to make an application to do that.

ME: Is that just something you're contemplating, or do you have an idea of where you want to go at this stage?

OJ: One never knows but I may well apply for a full-time position in due course but it's far too early at the moment. I don't know if I'd apply for silk in any event; it's a different world out there now in terms of the sort of work that silks do, particularly in my area of law.

ME: For kids coming through now, what sort of advice would you give to someone wanting to break into the legal profession, not necessarily exclusively becoming a barrister but the profession more generally - are there any top tips?

OJ: Yeah, there are two - one is go and do some work experience so you can see it, see what you're letting yourself in for, and the other is be prepared to work hard enough to get the grades because if you don't then it kind of falls apart, so you have to go and get the grades. You have to get your A levels or equivalent, you have to get your degree and you have to do well enough in them to get to the next stage.

ME: How important do you think it is then for kids to do work experience, not just work experience for understanding what the work would entail but also to network and get some real world understanding? Do you think that helps them with their overall interview skills, professional comportment etc?

OJ: I think that the benefits of work experience in terms of arming you for an interview are pretty limited from a pure skills, ability to do the job, perspective. But the number of candidates I see that haven't done work experience are incredibly limited, and so if you didn't do it, it's probably the one time that your work experience is queried because it would be so unusual to see a candidate that hadn't done anything that it would beg the question why not. There may well be very good reasons why not: I saw someone who had no means of support other than working while they studied so they didn't do work experience, they went and got a job - which was actually quite an impressive thing to do. Besides those sorts of situations, you do think why is this candidate not bothering, are they not that committed?

ME: What do you see as the general benefits of work experience?

OJ: For this profession, the Bar is very specialised and as such even the Bar school doesn't particularly prepare you very well for going on to whatever your practice will be at the Bar. So if you went off and spent time with a criminal practitioner or a commercial lawyer or something like that and then you came to me and interviewed it's not going to help hugely with family law. I think it's a good idea that you've seen them and then as a lawyer you have an idea of what you might want to do because there's nothing worse, and it does happen, that you invest years in a career path and then think, 'actually it's all a bit stressful, I don't like this type of work'. So I think that's where work experience is most valuable but will it turn them into a great candidate? We're going to spend a year training them in our specialised area through pupillage and what they'll learn in the first two weeks of that will put them well ahead of anything they could've learned elsewhere. The only exception to that is when we get candidates who have been paralegalling in the sort of specialist family law firms that instruct us and then they are seeing the same work. So that's helpful.

ME: Its absence is notable but its practical application isn't that useful?

OJ: Exactly. Although you do wonder about someone's commitment if they haven't bothered - because it's so easy to get a bit of work experience - you just have to go and ask basically.

ME: So it's fair to say, as good practice, it's necessary to help prove that this is a path that you want to embark on and whilst good for showing interest and developing soft skills don't expect it to prepare you for the rigour of the real world?

OJ: Exactly.

ME: Thank you.

2

THE DEVIL AND THE DEEP BLUE SEA

'If the grass is greener on the other side it's probably getting better care. Success is a matter of sticking to a set of common sense principles anyone can master.'

Earl Nightingale

People often talk about the grass being greener on the other side and there's probably some truth to that; it's the same reason I can't go for a meal with my wife without her swapping our plates over. No matter what choice you make, the alternative can always seem alluring - I suppose because once you've made the choice there's no mystery any more, just work. It's very easy to get distracted and much harder to stay the course but one of the key elements of career and academic planning is to keep going. If you've made a decision there's a reason you've made it but the lazy procrastinating brain worm is likely to look over your shoulder to see what might be more fun and try and rattle you. That's not to say that anything is final and decisions are irreversible but as we explored in the previous chapter it's worth examining the decision as coolly and rationally as possible. Don't go shopping hungry and don't reverse decisions just because things are getting hard or other things look shinier.

So what decisions do you have to make and what are the benefits? Simply put, you have five choices available to you when it comes to your academic/careers life post-school -

University
Traineeship/Apprenticeship
Gap Year
Work
Nothing

I'm assuming that if you're reading this book you're slightly more ambitious than considering doing nothing as a viable option, and going straight into the workforce without additional training is likely to limit your longer term options, so let's consider the other options available to you. Each has its merits and each has its downsides but no more is it the case that any option is better or worse - it's simply no longer true that university is the gold standard for future prospects. Most schools are pushing people towards them as that helps their position in the league tables, but doing the wrong degree or doing the right degree but in a terrible university is potentially more damaging to your future prospects than having a raft of relevant experience, letters of recommendation, professional contacts and a completed apprenticeship that you could achieve in the same three year period. On top of which, it in no way precludes you studying for a degree later in life alongside your work.

Too often in schools I have the same circular but never less than moronic conversation with teachers and headteachers about university. It's like it's been beaten into their heads that it should be university at any cost, regardless of whether it's remotely helpful or appropriate for your chosen career. The crazy thing is that both the poor quality of the advice and the circular conversations are in the best schools, often private schools where the expectation is that the advice would be the best available. One Head of Sixth at a high achieving school told me in no uncertain terms that any of the advice I had to offer would be redundant as '40 per cent of our students go on to Russell Group universities' - I asked her about the other 60 per cent.

That's not to denigrate university at all; I really believe in them and think they are splendid and wonderful institutions with lofty goals and everyone should have the opportunity to go and study if that is what they want. That said, people should not be made to feel lesser if they choose not to go: there is no one right way but there are a lot of wrong ways. Degrees are only as helpful as where you choose to apply yourself later on. I studied Art for heaven's sake - a lovely thing to be sure, but utterly useless for where I ended up.

Facts and figures

UNIVERSITY -
'To BA or not to BA; that is the question.'

Graduates:

- Are more likely to be employed than people leaving school with A levels or equivalent qualifications. They are also more likely to return to employment following any periods out of work.

- Are likely to earn 20-25 per cent more than those who leave education after secondary school level.

- Enjoy higher quality jobs than non-graduates.

- Enjoy better health outcomes, by being less likely to smoke, more likely to exercise, and less prone to depression.

- Have children who also benefit from the educational success of their parents: graduates tend to have a greater involvement with their child's education.

- Are more influential in the community, by being active citizens who are more likely to vote and participate in voluntary activities.

- Show positive attitudes towards diversity and equal opportunities, such as on race and gender equality issues.

- With higher levels of skill, are a source of wider innovation and economic growth.

UNIVERSITY –
Home or abroad?

Some rough comparisons just to show the comparative financial costs associated with UK, US and EU universities:

- Cambridge (UK) - Total: £18,210 p/a (Tuition = £9,250 p/a + £8,960 p/a living costs) Limited access to scholarships, bursaries, grants, etc. unless low-income.

- MIT (USA) - Total: in excess of $60,000 p/a (Tuition = $45,016 p/a) - However, they offer 'needs blind' admission (that is if they like you they'll find the money if you can't).

- Dutch universities (EU) - Total: c. £9,000 p/a (Tuition = £1,500 p/a) - Less 'up-front' assistance offered (e.g. loans & grants).

I don't know that it's particularly helpful for me to draw conclusions on some of these stats, for no other reason than that naturally for the full effect of these stats to be worth anything they have to have been monitoring non-graduates for a certain amount of time, and the changes that have occurred during that time as apprenticeships have caught up, which may significantly skew the life chances statistics. The key piece of information for me is that further education or training gives increased life chances rather than if you choose to end your learning journey after A-levels or equivalent.

Also the comparative costs of overseas study, something that, as we looked at earlier, is all too readily dismissed, does show that financially certain efficiencies can be achieved by making the decision to study elsewhere.

Alternatively you could seek out sponsored degrees - an increasingly popular way for companies to secure good people prior to the more competitive milk round and to breed loyalty by developing their own staff, essentially a school leaver scheme that ensures you get a degree as part of the programme.

Businesses that offer this include: Logica, Experian, Morrisons, PwC and many, many others.

As well as studying for a degree at university, students are often regarded as permanent employees of the company and receive a salary.

For example - NHS: certain allied health profession students on university courses leading to registration with the Health and Care Professions Council may be eligible for financial help from the NHS.

Eligible students accepted onto approved courses usually have their tuition fees paid in full and may receive financial support in the form of a bursary.

- They receive a £1,000 yearly grant

- They can apply for an additional means-tested bursary of up to £4,395 per year.

With universities, the critical thing, and one which is often overlooked by schools in their zeal to simply get you into a course, is that the planning for it needs to come much earlier than is standardly taught. The choices you make at GCSE will inform and in some cases actively dictate the options available to you at A level, which in turn will have a very specific impact on what course

you may choose to read at university.
We talked before about the importance of
decision making and how and why it is necessary
to make informed decisions regarding your
future and this is a perfect illustration of why.

Anecdotally, when I was at school, I took Economics at A level. I have no capacity for maths or science, numbers or formulae, which is why my parents were surprised when I told them - indeed they actively tried to discourage me, but, being fifteen, I knew better... I knew my future didn't lie in Economics but I was seduced by a persuasive sales technique from the teacher trying to bolster his first year's cohort. Not surprisingly I did very badly, but worse than that I persuaded my friend to do it as well and he dropped it after the first year, leaving him with two A levels. I mention this as it illustrates very clearly several key points.

One, the subjects you choose can and should work to serve a possible future. If you don't know what that future may yet be, there are good generalist subjects that will keep your options open. If you have a specific target, check with potential degree courses or apprenticeships what their requirements are.

Two, don't just pick your subjects on a whim - if university is in your grand plan then get as informed as possible about what they are looking for and make decisions that support that.

Three, don't be influenced by your friends, or you could end up on a wholly unsuitable course that will close off avenues to you.

If university is where you see yourself headed, make it your job to get as informed as possible, as early as possible, to understand what they are looking for and take steps to match your experiences and academic choices to those requirements. As of the time of writing, they have approved further price hikes on tuition fees: if you're going to pay them make sure it's worth it to you longer term.

Apprenticeships – 'You're hired!'

- **Not** just for those interested in construction or engineering as was traditionally the case.

- Can be undertaken in a huge number of different sectors and industries, from agriculture, law and accountancy to education, retail and art.

- Three different levels: intermediate apprenticeships, advanced apprenticeships and higher apprenticeships. It can take up to four years to reach the skill level required for a higher apprenticeship.

Why apprenticeships?

- **Learn while you earn:** Apprenticeships enable you to start working and earn a decent wage while you learn key skills and gain the qualifications future employers want. As your skills progress, your employer may up your pay cheque.

- **Paid holidays:** While on your apprenticeship, you'll be treated like a regular employee of the company in that you'll get a certain amount of paid holiday per year in addition to bank holidays.

- **Support:** One of the largest advantages of getting the qualifications you need in your field, while being able to put the skills you learn into practice at the same time, is that someone will always be on-hand to show you how things are done.

- **Good career prospects:** You will be working alongside and building relationships with your potential future employer. You are on their radar and having invested in you already will give you a good standing in their estimation when it comes to employing people.

- **Study** towards a related qualification (usually one day a week).

- Apprenticeships take one to four years to complete, depending on their level.

- **Traineeships** prepare young people, aged sixteen to twenty-four, and are designed to help students without the necessary skills or experience become 'work ready' and give them the skills to access a job or an apprenticeship.

- They provide the essential work preparation training, maths, English, and work experience needed to get an apprenticeship or other job.

- Training providers deliver traineeships, which are funded by the government, with employers providing the valuable work experience placement and interview as part of the programme.

Every week I see more and more 'prestige' businesses and companies across the spectrum embracing the apprenticeship model. In almost any sector you can find opportunities to get on the job, real world experience, and gain qualifications and be paid for doing so. If you're considering going to university solely to get a job where you can progress and make money, then for many careers an apprenticeship just gets you started that much quicker.

Gap Years – 'Please mind the gap.'

Some of you may not feel ready to go straight from school to university or into on the job training: if you're one of those, then a gap year is an entirely valid choice. Deferring entry until you've had an opportunity to discover who you are and what you want from life may well be the best use of your time if you are confused about what to do next. However, this is not to be confused with sitting around doing nothing for twelve months. A gap year, if used judiciously, will actually enhance your CV and hopefully give you a clearer understanding of what excites and drives you and could make you much more interesting as a person and as a potential student or employee.

There are lots of structured gap year providers offering you a wide range of choices from digging drainage ditches in Tanzania to volunteering at an orang-utan sanctuary in Borneo. Whatever it is you are interested in doing, there are options out there for you and the skills you'll learn - honing your language skills perhaps, working in a collegiate fashion, the simple act of exploring a world beyond yours - can be a real powerhouse statement of intent for a CV or application.

It may even be that you use that time to do re-sits and reapply for the right university or apprenticeship with more to say for yourself and better grades. Don't settle on the wrong thing for fear of missing the boat; a gap year is an entirely reasonable course of action and may better demonstrate your commitment and passion to a subject in the eyes of an admissions tutor or apprenticeship provider.

CASE STUDY

A client of mine, who was very bright and capable, with dreams of being a doctor from the age of twelve. She was someone who had done all the right things in terms of gaining additional experience by volunteering in labs etc. during the summer holidays from a relatively young age. Due to family circumstances she moved schools after her first year of A levels and had to change some of her options. Because of these changes she dropped a couple of grades on her predicted outcomes which went from being straight As to As & Bs. Her school, rather than encourage her to rely on the additional experiences that demonstrated her commitment, encouraged her to opt for a business degree at one of the worst universities in the country. Panicked, she accepted it. After I spent some time with her we decided it would be better to see what her actual grades were rather than the vague predicted grades, take a year out to volunteer in labs and overseas medical charity work, and reapply for the following year. This was a classic case of the school scaremongering and getting someone to give up on a long-held dream in favour of a short term gain for their position in the league tables.

CONCLUSION - Don't give up on your dream because someone with a vested interest in seeing you tick boxes has told you you're wrong to have that dream. Don't compromise on your life for someone else's convenience. Another option for her would have been to apply for a degree in Bio-Chemistry and do Medicine as a graduate or Bio-medicine/Biomedical Science and transfer after her first year. There are always alternative routes, and before you accept the so-called wisdom of your advisors make it your business to check these out; no one will ever care as much about your life as you, so do your research!

3

KNOW THYSELF

'If most of us remain ignorant of ourselves it
is because self- knowledge is painful and we
prefer the pleasures of illusion.'

Aldous Huxley

Some of you will be learning to drive or about to; others will already have passed - one of the first things you will have learnt (or will) is what to do in the event of a skid. Common sense would suggest you steer away from it but in reality that just makes the wheels lock up. What you actually need to do is steer into the skid. But wait, I hear you cry, this isn't a guide to faultless driving in treacherous weather conditions. No, it is not and I congratulate you on having picked this up. However, it doesn't make it less true and it is an entirely acceptable metaphor, so what do I mean by steering into the skid? Don't go against the grain, play to your strengths, don't swim against the tide. I think that covers what I mean and exhausts all other trite metaphors.

You will already have natural skills, aptitudes and interests, some of which you are actively aware of and others which are there but you have yet to identify, and it is for this reason that self-knowledge is so critical to the effective planning of your career and academic goals. If you hate people and working in an office, no matter how hard you try, working around lots of people in an office environment is always going to be soul-sucking and terrible. The choices you make should support a range of options whose outcomes don't involve working with people in an office, and that's what I mean by steering into the skid; you can't be what you're not and trying is often going to be horrible and painful and a waste of your time. Happiness in work isn't a given of course, but it doesn't mean that at this stage you shouldn't at least strive for the possibility. Remember, you're young. Don't compromise on your ambitions when you don't have to.

The path to self-knowledge can be difficult and painful, but like anything worth doing it was always going to be that way. Before you can block out a career path you need to be supremely self-critical: you need to be honest with yourself in a way that probably won't make you feel very good but it's a whole lot better than having someone else be that brutal with you. For instance I wanted to be a comic book artist when I was younger (who am I kidding? I still do) but, try as I might, I simply wasn't good enough and, because I was arrogant enough to ignore that little voice in the back of my head, I still pursued Art at university with no real idea of how I was going to turn that into a career. Inevitably I didn't become a comic book artist and I rather squandered my time, time which has taken me a long time to claw back. I suppose I might've given myself a better chance of success if I had networked and tried to get internships etc but that's for another chapter. The point is, you need to understand who you are and where your abilities and interests lie. If your parents always wanted you to be a lawyer, no problem, but be really sure it's what you want as well; don't do it because they were lawyers and it's just what's expected of you. Do it because you genuinely love it.

So, let's do a breakdown of the different considerations when it comes to self-knowledge.

APTITUDE - (noun) a natural ability to do something; a natural tendency.

This is what we need you to identify. This is the proverbial skid I was talking about before. It's the manifestation of who you are, what defines you - your innate abilities. Everyone's got something, maybe it's sport, maybe it's debate, drawing, languages, influencing people, listening skills, acting. Whatever it is, whatever you are and whoever you are, there is one thing you can do better than other people you know.

Through self-knowledge and reflection you can identify what that thing is (if you haven't already) and you can develop that to become an advantageous selling point that you can use. The biggest scandal is when you have a natural aptitude and refuse to use it and develop it properly, which is where we come to...

SKILL - (mass noun) - the ability to do something well; expertise.

It actually comes from an old Norse word which is more akin to knowledge. Knowledge of an area, really knowing something. Skill is an aptitude that has been developed. To take my cartooning as an example, I had a talent for it and I practised lots and lots, and over time that aptitude was developed into a skill - you'll have no doubt picked up on my totally boss drawings smattered across the pages. Now, many of you may think you are without skills, but that almost certainly isn't true; it simply means it's either undercooked right now or you've yet to identify it as such. When you're at school it's very hard to shake off that kind of institutional thinking that accompanies every conversation about your future: by that I mean how what you do can be equated to a tangible educational result. Being good at writing is associated with English Language, a flair for languages would see you being encouraged to do French or German or Spanish. Good at adding? Maths is the thing for you. Only that's very short-termist, short-sighted and wrong-headed, and students are press-ganged into academic choices without a focus on the bigger scheme of things. You may be good at certain academic choices that would naturally map onto a variety of career choices but equally you might be unremarkable in lessons but have a wealth of skills that your school doesn't know how to harness effectively the skill to command or lead a group of people such as in sports or the Duke of Edinburgh Award, or in the CCF or in a school society; the skill to work with people in a collaborative and productive way; the skill to persuade and influence; an entrepreneurial ability that doesn't conform to a specific academic subject - these are all skills, useful skills, that can be used effectively in the real world and should be nurtured not dismissed.

Maybe you have a logical bent of mind that means you are particularly good at problem solving, there's some maths in there, maybe a nod to the sciences, but it's fundamentally just an ability you have that if used often in everyday scenarios can be parlayed into a career in something like Project Management or Logistics. So, if you look at that as an end point and work back from it, a path can be revealed to you that wouldn't necessarily suggest itself from your current vantage point of thinking about what subject to study.

INTEREST - (mass noun) the feeling of wanting to know about something or someone.

It almost naturally follows that your interests will be aligned with your skills and aptitudes: if you love playing football it's unlikely that you won't also enjoy watching it and discussing it with your friends. If you enjoy drawing and painting, chances are you have a favourite artist and will enjoy going to galleries. If you like writing you're going to like reading. Having an interest in a subject - or rather, an area - is how we can begin to define where your skills and aptitudes may take you. By taking an interest in an area you are more likely to turn up possible career paths, even inadvertently. That's why it's so important to foster your interests - your parents and school may see them as a distraction from your exams but what your unconscious mind is doing is, very possibly, giving you the biggest signposts towards where your goals may lie.

Now we've identified what we mean by each of these words, how do they relate to self-knowledge and why is it so important? The important thing to realise is that not everyone who enjoys playing football is going to make it to the premiership, and not every cartoonist is going to draw for Marvel, but that doesn't mean to say you can't still carve a career for yourself in a field that will be a whole lot more fulfilling than something which doesn't excite you. There's a very old thought exercise which asks the question, 'If money wasn't an issue what job would you do?' - obviously the thinking is flawed because money is always an issue if you want to have things and pay for those little luxuries like food and electricity, but it does raise a valid point: stop thinking about your expectations from life for a moment and think about what you'd genuinely love to do - it'll be something that speaks to your interests, skills and aptitudes.

So, to follow the football idea, if it's what you love, be honest with yourself - are you going to play in the premiership? Probably not - by the time you read this you would likely already know that - so stop pretending it's a possibility and think around the problem. Coaching, refereeing, something in sports management? Could you study overseas and get a scholarship to do so in a country where the sport is played at lower level - the USA, Canada, Australia? All of these are options for you, but the sad truth is people give up too easily. By understanding what the limitations of your abilities are you can afford to get creative; where others might see the end of the road, look beyond it and see where else your skills may take you.

The single biggest issue people have, as I've mentioned above, is failing to recognise their aptitudes as aptitudes and rather just dismissing them as stuff they're okay at. Self-knowledge isn't innate; it's something you have to work at and sometimes disproving ideas is as helpful as proving them. A lot of people might believe they have a clear view of what they want to do based on the biased decision-making processes we explored in Chapter 1, that is to say you might think you want to do something because you just feel like you want to do something, or your parents want you to do something, or your school or the society you were born into suggests that it's the right thing to do. This is flawed thinking: a decision that has been made in a vacuum without any external or corroborating evidence.

STATEMENT: I want to be a lawyer.

How do you know this? Have you worked in a solicitors' office? Done a mini-pupillage at a chambers? Volunteered at the Citizens Advice Bureau? On what basis are you making this decision? No one is born with an aptitude for the law because that's a manufactured construct. If the answer is, 'I understand what the profession entails and I want to make money' that's an entirely acceptable position, but unless you've had direct experience of a certain industry it's very hard to know how you'll feel about it in reality rather than in the abstract. So, you need to dig deeper and really examine your motivations. If you accept that until you've engaged with the reality of a job it's hard to know what it entails, let alone whether you would really enjoy it. That only leaves the money. You can earn money in any number of professions, so why law? Is that your aptitude? Are you good at debating? Do you have a deep sense of moral purpose? Do you feel compelled to do some good in the world, work for a charity from a legal perspective? Do you like the idea of a high stakes negotiation because you thrive on conflict and you like matching wits? These are more honest questions and that's where you need to get to. By being truly honest with yourself about your aptitudes, you can identify what your motivations truly are. That in turn can help promote a certain career path and one whereby you can create a much more compelling argument about what you can offer an employer or admissions tutor, because it's honest and passionate and more nuanced than simply saying "I want to be a lawyer." Moreover, by identifying what your motivation is you potentially open up a much wider range of jobs that will speak directly to that motivation and instinct, rather than simply trying to shoehorn yourself into a role that superficially makes sense. Or you just may really, really want to be a lawyer.

The point of the above case study is simply to highlight that sometimes even the things you think you want might have unconscious biases attached to them, and by being really honest with yourself about certain issues you might uncover likes and dislikes that you didn't even know you felt.

As important as it is to understand what positive attributes and capacities you have, it is equally important to understand how far those abilities may take you - we've all watched deluded nutters on the X Factor who truly believe they have what it takes to fill arenas and we all know that the closest they'll get to that is some disinterested passers-by booing them busking on the streets. Not everyone can be famous or feted and that's okay. If you like singing, join a choir, form a band, play with your mates, maybe even gig a little, but have a back-up plan just in case. I could've spent my life doodling and trying to make it as an artist but I think at a certain point you have to be honest with yourself and own the fact that you may not have what it takes at this stage in your life; you can then enjoy it as a hobby and get on with the business of forging a path that will pay the bills as well as make you happy. That is where the brutal honesty has to come in. I'm not saying don't pursue your dreams and I'm not saying listen to the cynics and people who tell you it won't happen. You should absolutely pursue your dreams, but give yourself a time frame, don't go looking for the end of the rainbow - you need to be hard on yourself, you may be an undiscovered genius but you have to accept the possibility that you might not be. Once you accept that possibility, put plan B into place; this isn't an admission of failure, it's a proactive decision to take control of your life and not let others define your worth. Plus you can still pursue your dreams in your spare time.

Some of the greatest discoveries and most inspiring stories from business have come about through accident or failure: sometimes plan B takes you exactly where you were supposed to be, even if it doesn't feel that way when you set off.

EXAMPLE - Harrison Ford, one of the most bankable and successful film stars of all time, thanks to *Star Wars* and *Indiana Jones*, at one point was the star of six of the top ten highest grossing films of all time. He had pretty much given up on his goal of acting after years toiling in anonymity on non-speaking bit parts. He became a carpenter and that was how he earned his living, that was his plan B, and he supported his wife and kids - that wasn't an admission of failure, just a pragmatic decision that he couldn't rely on the possibility of making it big as an actor. He ended up doing some set building at the studios and caught the attention of a casting director who thought he had something and began championing him to directors. His plan B, by happy accident, gave him the break he had been looking for. He didn't get his first starring role, which was *Star Wars*, until the age of thirty-five. That's a long time to wait, and he quite rightly pursued a job that he enjoyed and would pay the bills, but that didn't mean giving up on his dreams, dreams which he eventually fulfilled.

CASE STUDY

DAVID MOONEY

David Mooney is the owner/director of Carwood Catering, a north-west based chain of gastro pubs and a craft bakery. He is a regular contributor on local TV and radio as resident chef and fronted his own TV show for Granada called Food Hunter. He began his training as a chef after spending a summer in France that turned into two years and coming back to work with Raymond Blanc and Marco-Pierre White before striking out on his own.

ME: What first drew you into the industry?

DM: I've always loved food. Growing up in a very, very ordinary suburb in Greater Manchester, it's not your first thought. Your mates are talking about becoming brickies and plumbers and all sorts of things like that. I always, always loved the way food started from this raw product and turned into an edible product, and how that process worked both from a sciencey point but also a creative point of view. That was it really. I started out working front of house and realised that wasn't all I wanted to do.

ME: Thinking about your schooling, were you academic as such or did you turn your back on that because you knew this is where you wanted to be? How did it go from being a passion to being a career?

DM: I ended up going to a nice respectable boarding school in Yorkshire, which I absolutely loved - the whole ethos of it. It was quite progressive, so you were given options, and I wasn't pushed towards the sciences but rather the languages, and the slightly more artistic things - history a bit, little bit of art itself but I can't draw a stick man. But much to my regret I left school pretty much as soon as I could. I wish I'd stayed on and done my A levels, just to prove to myself that I could have done them. I won't say regret but you do wonder what your life might've been like. For the sake of two years - it seemed like an eternity at sixteen, but at fifty-three not so much!

ME: You left at sixteen. What did you do next?

DM: Well, I'm lucky enough to have a French side to my family: I have an aunt and a cousin who are both French. My French aunt married my uncle - sadly he's no longer with us, but in the holidays before my O Levels - God, that ages me - I went over to practise my French oral, my French speaking, and I met a guy who had a very rustic, very simple restaurant in rural France, in the middle of nowhere. It was a converted cowshed and he asked if I wanted to come back in the summer and I ended up staying two years. That was where my food education blossomed, because I ended up working on a market garden. We'd pick the tomatoes in the afternoon, pack them up, and in the morning we'd take them to market to sell them, and it was that simple, it was that parochial, that's how it happened. You know, there were courgettes, peppers, cucumber - I still remember it like it was yesterday; it was hard work but I loved it. To grow this stuff, I remember old women fighting about the last tomatoes, it was that well thought of, that's when I fell in love with the produce. That's the most important thing about food, you've got to start

with the best produce, whether it's a potato,
onion, piece of foie-gras. You have to start
with the best you can afford, you have to love it,
you have to feel passionately about food and
wine to do this job. Otherwise it's easy to get
cynical about it when you've done a seventeen
hour day. So, I came back and worked for
Raymond Blanc, along with Marco-Pierre White,
doing ridiculous high-end, two Michelin star
cooking. The pressure was insane though, just
unreal, and after doing that for two years I knew
that wasn't what I wanted to do, so I came home
to the family business.

ME: When you came back to the family business did
you have a grand plan about where you wanted to
go, the direction you wanted your career to go?

DM: When I came back the business had plateaued.
It was a very, very traditional high end French
restaurant, with God knows how many tablecloths
and how many knives and forks, and silver plates
and salt and peppers and all that sort of shizzle.
I knew I didn't want to do that. I wasn't sure
what I wanted to do so it was probably a couple
of years after that that I then realised that what
I wanted to do was the same standard of food
but in a much more casual environment, more
of a sort of brasserie. I don't want to sound like
I rode in on a white horse, but the business
was going nowhere fast and changing to a light
brasserie style, still with the same standards -
still bought everything fresh, made bread
every day, made desserts every day and all
that sort of thing - and it was just an absolute
rampant success.

ME: Was that the end of the line in terms of your thinking was it just a case of we need to turn the business around? Or did you see it as a springboard for something bigger?

DM: To be honest with you I wanted to take that concept around the country.,Unfortunately around that time, there was that chain called *Cafe Rouge*, who had a huge amount of money behind them; it was a stylised version of what I did. I mean the food's bloody awful but they were opening everywhere, railways stations, high streets and all the rest of it. I just didn't have any experience of how to grow a brand, how to finance the growing of a brand. I didn't have any support behind me. You know, my parents were at an age where they weren't really looking to take risks and all the rest of it. So it was all a bit... yeah. So we just sort of sat on it for about fifteen years. We had a couple of pubs and that was great to be part of that gastro pub revolution and they did very well. But again, I really wanted to open probably a dozen of those and be sat on the terrace of my little cottage in the South West of France being a millionaire, but hey ho.

ME: The TV and media stuff, was that just to further market you and your brand? Did you see it as a way to promote the wider business or was it something you had aspirations in anyway?

DM: I'd love to say it was part of the plan but it was just a conversation that took place with a guy from Granada. They were doing a year-long charity event and part of that was doing a cookbook, the *Life Challenge*, and they came and did some of the chefs *in situ* as it were, took photographs of them and everything, and some did little bits to go out on the local station, and off the back of that they came over at the end of it and just said, 'you were quite natural there. Do you want to do some more stuff?' and I said, 'yeah, fine, that'd be great.' That metamorphosed into a couple of series for them and then I was the chef on the local news station which went out at half six every night for two or three years. The TV was ticking along. I was doing three or four things a week, and it was just a great way to have a couple of holidays a year. The people I worked with have all got their own deals and stuff but I never saw it as a means to an end, I just saw it as a bit of fun that could get a few people into the restaurant.

ME: What advice would you give any young person wanting to get into this career?

DM: I would say get the basic knowledge of all areas of the business. Go and work in a decent kitchen for six and a half months, go and work in a decent dining room for six to twelve months, go and work in a hotel for six to twelve months and understand what makes this business work. It's not simply a matter of getting a bag of carrots, chopping them up and serving them, there's so much more to it than that. The thing is, it's not one thing done massively well, it's a thousand things done well, and you have to understand that. As Bernard Shaw said, 'youth is wasted on the young'. You have to realise that potentially every weekend, if you work in your local pub you can get promoted, go further, to suggest things and get to do things. I'm not saying be cocky about it but just be a sponge and from sixteen to eighteen to twenty just soak it all up. At that age no one's going to give you a lease to a building or give you a load of money to open your own place; what you need to do is just be a sponge and learn every aspect of the business from the best people you can.

4

GOOOOOOOOOOAAAAALLLLL!

'Dream as if you'll live forever, live as if
you'll die today.'
James Dean

'It always seems impossible until it's done.'
Nelson Mandela

This chapter is all about the importance of goal-setting, short, medium and long term goals, how to hold yourself accountable and what kind of goals you need to be setting yourself that will stretch you but won't break you.

So, if we take as a goal 'I want to be Batman', that would seem naturally ridiculous but it does serve a point; Bruce Wayne did not become Batman overnight, nor did he do it on a whim. He was motivated and had a goal but along the way he had lots of other goals, from training himself to fight, designing a dudey costume, becoming the world's greatest detective, learning to fly, stunt drive and free dive. Any single thing he can do is the result of intense practice and training and it's as true for a fictional figure as it is for someone like Wayne Rooney or Steve Jobs, or anyone in the public eye, or a judge, or an Olympic athlete, or the best accountant in a local practice. Success, however you choose to define that, is not a happy accident. It is the inevitable by-product of doing the right things well and setting goals.

What do I need to do?

Well, I'm glad you asked that - obviously every journey is an entirely individual one so I'm going to map out a specific journey towards one goal, but the principles are consistent no matter what you want to do, where you want to live or what you want to accomplish.

The first thing you need to do is try and figure out some kind of end point: it doesn't have to be a job *per se* but one thing, one idea that you can't shake off. Something that excites you about your future - it could be anything from the car you want to drive, to the kind of house or even the country you want to live in. Whatever it is, whatever material or otherwise ambition you have, we can take that and park it. That's our tether. That's the stake in the ground that we will keep coming back to.

For the purposes of working through an example I will say that my goal is to live in New York. At this stage I don't know precisely what I want to do when I'm there but that's my tether. In order to support that goal I need to work logically back from that point to understand what I need to do in order to get there.

DAY 1

Short term goal
Find out about visa requirements

Medium term goal
Learn more about the city

Long term goal
Live in New York

Now these seem pretty easy short and medium term goals and that's very much the point of the exercise at this stage. The worst thing you can do is set unachievable goals. By breaking it down into task-oriented, bite-size pieces, it's much easier to set yourself realistic tasks - all of which build towards the long term goal.

For the next stage, you have your goals, now you need to set certain parameters to ensure that you don't keep it putting it off. One of the favourite acronyms doing the rounds is the SMART objective system. For each letter of the acronym there is, basically, the equivalent of a beginner, intermediate and expert version. This is to avoid stagnation. The moment your goals become too easy they become meaningless - this little aide memoire can be just the ticket to keep you progressing.

SMART

S - specific, significant, stretching

M - measurable, meaningful, motivational

A - agreed upon, attainable, achievable, acceptable, action-oriented

R - realistic, relevant, reasonable, rewarding, results-oriented

T - time-based, time-bound, timely, tangible, trackable

The T is possibly the most important aspect, a goal without an end point is just a meaningless to-do list.

My short term goal is to understand the visa requirements for living in the USA. I will give myself this evening in order to do some research on this.

My medium term goal is to learn more about the city. This goal needs to be defined further because watching *Friends* probably doesn't qualify. I need to redefine that goal in order to meet the SMART requirements. So, we will change that to: I will research which areas of the city are safest to live in and may cater towards my interests more. I will do this within the next seven days.

My long term goal is to live in New York - this hasn't changed yet but maybe I've begun to think about when I want that to happen.

DAY 2

Armed with the knowledge of visa restrictions from Day 1's research, I will have learned that probably the easiest way to get to live in the city is to either get a student visa or get sponsorship from a business to go and work there. My short term goal has now changed: I need to look into student visa programmes and studying in New York. Given that I am a school leaver it's unlikely I will get sponsorship from a business as I'm not currently ready to join the workforce. My medium term goal of understanding the city remains the same but with more focus. Which universities are in the city and which run courses that I can meet the standard of and do something that interests me?

SHORT TERM GOAL
Look into specifically student visas

MEDIUM TERM GOAL
Research universities in the city

LONG TERM GOAL
Live in New York

Again I will take the night to research student visas and give myself seven days to research universities.

DAY 3

I now have a pretty good idea of the student visa system and have confirmed that the best way to get over there is to study at one of the universities. I don't know much about them and what they offer but I have begun to look at the options and have identified Columbia, New York University (NYU), City University of New York (CUNY), State University of New York (SUNY), Julliard Music School and New York Film Academy, amongst others. Some of these will self-select as we move forward, given my limited interest in certain specialities.

SHORT TERM GOAL

Look at the universities I shortlisted

MEDIUM TERM GOAL

Identify where the unis are vs where
I want to live in the city

LONG TERM GOAL

Live in New York

DAY 4

So, I've discounted a couple of the universities based on their specialities. I'm not headed to Julliard as I can't play an instrument and I'm no Spielberg so the Film Academy is out. That leaves me with a few choices - NYU, SUNY, CUNY and Columbia. I've also seen that Columbia is based up in Spanish Harlem and whilst extremely prestigious, the area, frankly, scares me a little and I'm not sure I'm Ivy League material, so I'm plumping for NYU based on its reputation and location. This helps me refine my thinking a little bit further. I know I want to go to study at NYU in order to achieve my goal of living in New York but what do I want to do there and, more importantly, what do they offer?

SHORT TERM GOAL

Look at NYU courses

MEDIUM TERM GOAL

Look at course requirements, and extra-
curricular activities they look at favourably

LONG TERM GOAL

Live in New York

DAY 5

Thinking more about my skills, aptitudes and interests as identified previously I have started to think about possible courses that would be interesting and would make sense given my academic record to date. Also thinking longer term, New York is a very expensive city to live in, so beyond studying there this degree needs to potentially lead to a career that pays well - this will help further refine my search.

SHORT TERM GOAL

Working within the parameters of my current studies, interests and potential earnings which courses support my long term goal?

MEDIUM TERM GOAL

Look into bursaries and scholarships available to overseas students and ones that may be attached to certain courses

LONG TERM GOAL

Live in New York

DAY 6

I've settled on architecture. I'm doing art and design already and the earning potential is there, plus with big name firms worldwide the possibility of getting sponsorship to stay afterwards is pretty strong.

SHORT TERM GOAL

Identify local architect firms that can give me work experience

MEDIUM TERM GOAL

Secure an internship at a local architectural
practice during my next half term/holiday

LONG TERM GOAL

Live in New York

Obviously this could go on and on until I'm a successful architect living in a Manhattan loft but what it hopefully does is provide a basis for your own thinking. By setting tangible and realistic goals, even little ones like 'Google some stuff', within a very short space of time you have the beginnings of a workable plan to help you achieve your goal. I purposely didn't choose a career at the beginning of the exercise to emphasise the point that even if you don't have really concrete goals regarding a certain career, by working logically back from an end point you can uncover options simply by selecting or deselecting from the options available to you once you have a wider goal in place.

Research and goal-setting go hand in hand. By understanding what is required of you to reach your tether point you are able to set sensible and realistic goals. It's no good simply saying 'I want to live in New York' and then buying a plane ticket. That is where the research comes in, and little by little you challenge your assumptions about what's needed to reach your goal and start taking the necessary steps towards it becoming a reality.

You'll see that the medium term goals adapt and react to whatever you learn in your short term goal's research and that's fine. These things are necessarily fluid and as long as your tether remains the same and the focus is unchanged it's okay to play with these bits so that it remains fit for purpose - like a shark, you should always be moving forward.

Obviously, your example will be much different to the one I've detailed and the nature of your goals may also differ radically, but no matter what your aspirations are, securing and locking on to a tether can be an invaluable way of logically plotting a series of small goals.

Checklist for goal setting

No matter who you are or what your circumstances are there will be one thing that pops into your head when you close your eyes and picture your ideal future. So, close your eyes and think about what that thing is.

It's important to temper that dream with at least a side order of cynicism - impossible goals are good, implausible ones less so. I'm not going to be Batman, no matter how many small goals I might set myself.

Now you've got that thing firmly in your mind, logically work back from that end point. This is important; there are lots of choices and lots of different routes towards that same goal and there's no one right way. That said, there will be certain universal truths: if you want a big house in London or a flash car or to live overseas you will have to make choices that can demonstrably be in service of that goal.

Don't over-reach with your short term goals: softly softly catch a monkey, as the meaningless expression goes. Start small, a bit of research, a conversation, whatever it is; don't overwhelm yourself; that's the surest way to be discouraged and give up on the whole thing before you've even started.

Make sure you give yourself a time limit and hold yourself to account: by setting small and realistic goals you can accomplish them within the time limits you set; plus a time limit, as arbitrary as it might be, does tend to focus the mind.

Constantly reassess your short and medium term goals - are you being a busy fool or is this pro-actively moving you towards your long term goal? Don't be distracted by irrelevancies that may be easier to deal with than the real tasks you've set yourself.

Don't settle. If you've a long term goal, give it your all. Halfway there may be great but no one gets compliments for half cooking a chicken or putting one shoe on.

CASE STUDY

DR. BARRY J. GIBB PHD

A PhD doctorate who worked as a research scientist at University College London's prestigious Wolfson Institute for Biomedical Research. Now the celebrated author of The Rough Guide to the Brain and an award winning documentary maker working with the Wellcome Trust as their Science Multimedia Producer interviewing the likes of Sir David Attenborough.

ME: Perhaps we could start with your just telling me a bit about your educational background?

BG: I started at Dens Road Primary School and then I went to Morgan Academy which was a comprehensive and yeah, I suppose I showed an aptitude for science, although at the time I didn't think of it as science. I just liked finding stuff out.

ME: Did your scientific/academic bent reveal itself to you very early? Did you particularly embrace it, or was it a case of, 'there's a possible career here' or was it more something you had an abiding interest in, that you came to think I can make a career of it?

BG: Ah, okay. I see. I have probably never in my life considered the idea of a career. At Morgan Academy I just really liked science, and in particular I liked Biology and Maths and there came a point at school, despite my love for both of these subjects, it became apparent that because of the curriculum I couldn't follow them both. It was a bit frustrating because at one point, because of my schedule, they tried to get me to do things like cake decoration and stuff. But no, I just sort of pursued them and when it basically came to an age where you choose a university it simply wasn't an option for me not to go really. Principally because I was just really interested in it, but I was the first person in my family to go to university.

ME: Do you think that's what informed your decision, because of parental pressure to go, or was it something you were interested in doing because you were genuinely interested in doing it and they created an atmosphere that was supportive of that?

BG: Yeah, I think at that time in your life when you've done your GCSEs and stuff like that and you appear to have an aptitude for things, I suppose relative to a lot of the other people, I was quite academic. Going to university just felt like the thing to do and it was also a way of putting off this awful thing called getting a job. I went to university purely as an intellectual exercise in learning more about stuff that I was interested in. There was never a point at which I was thinking about a career itself and my folks were supportive of it but also didn't quite know what to make of it to an extent. Because they hadn't been to university, I think when I came home I was always quite conscious to not play it up in a sense. I didn't want to be a smart arse in my own house so I just sort of kept my head down and studied and did the things that really, really appealed to me. Initially it was psychology but biochemistry was the one that really just stood out: there was something about the fact that it was so absolutely bursting with facts and information about the mechanism of life that it really appealed to me. So I pursued that with vigour, then, over the years - it was a very competitive university by the way - Dundee had a very good reputation for biochemistry and I was also surrounded by people who really liked getting good marks. I remember it was incredibly intense and I didn't like the competitive nature but, you know, I suppose played along with it a little bit and did try to excel and in the end I did get a first class degree from that. So, that was the university phase.

ME: At what point did you go from pursuing it as a purely academic exercise and start to think longer term about whether this was going to become your career or was it more feeling your way and seeing where it went?

BG: Well, the people at university were very keen for me to do a PhD after my degree, but I didn't really want to, partly because of that sort of pressure cooker environment that I'd been in, particularly for the last year I just thought I'd had it with all of that stuff and at the time I was in a relationship and she was going down to London so I thought, oh, I'll do that. I guess because I thought, 'I've got science, I'll try and get a job.' So I ended up getting a job with Smith Kline Beecham, which was a big pharma down there and of course because I had absolutely no knowledge of London geography I ended up commuting about five hours a day. I was living in and working in a completely different area of greater London. So I did that for about fourteen months, working on asthma and another disease which I can't remember. It was quite interesting because it was academic but it was also a very business-focused mentality. I thought 'okay, this is kind of interesting,' but I was struck by, relative to the degree, how different the culture was to one of pure learning.

I wasn't entirely sure it was a great fit for me so I resigned and the opportunity to do some work abroad came up. My partner at the time was doing a degree in languages so it became apparent that it would involve her spending some time in Berlin and in Mexico. So, what I did was engineer a situation where I could also work in those places too, and in Berlin I managed to get a job in a lab. So, what was interesting for me, I suppose career-wise there, is that it was a purely academic lab. It was the Max Delbruck Centre for Molecular Medicine; there were just a really interesting bunch of people and that was my first experience of research. It was simultaneously relaxed but also intellectually intense and I kind of liked that 'vibe' for want of a better word; it just sat well with me. So, I did that for a few months and then went off to Mexico and taught English for a few months [laughs] - the reason I'm laughing is because I remember holding a conversation with my class about serial killers and I remember thinking, 'this is just the most surreal thing I've ever done', but it was just to earn money. They were so incredibly grateful for anybody who was prepared to show up and talk English, and that was great.

Whilst I was out there, I started to think - and I was strongly influenced by my time in Berlin - I thought 'I think I'm going to do a PhD.' The fear of that super-intense academic environment had dwindled and I felt like, 'I kind of enjoy finding

out stuff' and being independent was a big factor
- increasingly I came to realise that my nature
lends itself to independent pursuits, so the idea
of effectively tinkering on a problem in a lab
just felt quite nice to me. So I applied for PhD
and I got one working with a guy called Chris
Miller who was working in Denmark Hill at the
Institute of Psychiatry. I worked with him for
three years, got the PhD; that was interesting.
I suppose at that time I did have a really strong
passion for science and I did enjoy it a lot, doing
the PhD. It wasn't for the pursuit of the PhD,;
all of these titles, these bits of paper don't mean
anything to me - I just enjoyed the act of trying
to figure stuff out.

Then I did a post-doc which showed an entirely
different side to academic science, one driven by
intellectual property and business. This skewed
my sense of what academic research was and I
ended up in this lab environment for two years,
which was ultra-competitive and driven by profit
and I just thought 'I didn't sign up for this,' so
I resigned again [laughs]. This time I ended up
working in another lab, this time at UCL at The
Wolfson Institute of Biomedical Research.,Tthat
was great, that was working with John Garthwaite.
What was lovely about that is that he didn't have
anybody doing what I could do, which technically
was called molecular biology, so I just went into
that lab as the only molecular biologist and just
set all that up for him. Which was brilliant
because my confidence at the time was low
because of the previous post-doc and he was really
welcoming and really supportive. Then I met my
new partner, Charmaine, there; it just felt like
this was really working.

ME: And you met me there as well - let's not forget that. I mean Charmaine's great but you know...

BG: [Laughs]. That is clearly, I mean obviously, one of the highlights of my life.

ME: And your career I would think?

BG: And my career. [Laughs]. So, I worked with John for about five years. I think one of the great attractions of science is that it speaks to your curiosity, pursuing problems, stuff like that and I had been working on pretty much the same problem for about five years, so I was just getting to the point where it was getting a bit stale. I remember around that time I was getting really interested in more creative pursuits. I mean I didn't get paid for any of this stuff but I was doing a bit of writing on the side, publishing stuff online and the Naked Scientists was quite a popular science comms [communicating scientific content for a non-science audience] broadcast organisation and they were putting my stuff up online.

That was the first time in my life that anyone said to me that I was good at writing, because I had no idea whether I could do it or not. I thought actually I kind of like this. The sort of writing I was doing was taking an idea from science but very specifically writing it for lay people, people like my Mum and Dad, who were probably interested in the world but didn't have any scientific background and definitely didn't know any of the jargon. So, I pursued that and through that got into the idea of film-making. Largely because there was this guy who came into work and he was showing us all these new films he'd been making about his new baby and I was completely disinterested [laughs] in the baby footage but I thought 'holy shit, he's managed to do all this on this little digital camera,' and that was a bit of a turning point. I immediately thought (because I tend to be quite black and white) 'I am going to get a computer, I am going to start editing and making films' and that was it, basically.

I started going to film festivals, still working in science, but I started going to film festivals and started trying to soak up the culture and thinking of film-makers to get my head around what was and wasn't possible, because at the time I had these notions... Sam Raimi was always a big hero of mine, so I was thinking 'yeah I'm going to make the next *Evil Dead* film' or something like that. But yeah, it was a bit of a reality check. I thought okay, and started reading books by David Lynch, and the guy who did *El Mariachi*, Robert Rodriguez.

ME: Rebel without a crew?

BG: Exactly, rebel without a crew. I began to think - you know what, I probably could do a lot at some point but at the moment the reality is that single people like me with a camera tend to make documentaries. I started trying to make documentaries and I dabbled with it, and experimented with it all the while I was still working in the lab, I taught myself how to edit on the very first version of Final Cut Pro and I was using archive footage and I was making mash-ups to basically take old footage and then re-edit it in a way that changes the meaning. I was basically doing it to entertain myself. I would take these old public information films and re-edit them to say the inverse of what they intended to say, just for fun. It had a very serious purpose though, in the sense that it helped me understand how editing worked and how to use the software.

From then on, I just hit a blank at the lab because I was now thinking much more about film than I was about the science, and I was now married to my partner and she, well, my parents' reaction was that they thought I was mad to give up this amazing career in science but Charmaine was very supportive and for five years I basically just tried to build incrementally. I tried to turn myself from a scientist into someone who would get paid to write and make films about science.

Things I did in that time, I did a short film. There was an office called the British Association for the Advancement of Science and they had an event coming up about stem cells and I knew someone who worked for the BA so I said 'well, if you don't mind I'll make this film for you, just a little four minute thing to kickstart the night's conversation' and she said, 'yeah, go for it'. So I got my camera, I went up to Newcastle. No one paid me anything for this at the time, I just did it because I really wanted to see if I could do and I kind of recognised the fact was no-one was going to take me seriously as a film-maker unless I had something they could see. So I went and did some filming around where I lived, interviewing some locals about stem cells research and that kind of stuff. I came back, put it together and they really liked it and they did actually pay me retrospectively for that which was very kind of

them. Weirdly there was a person from the British
Council there and he came up to me afterwards
and he said, 'we really liked that. Could you do a
thing, almost identical to that but on the subject
of carbon emissions in cities?' I was like, Yes!
That was my first professional job in the sense
that it was properly paid which was great.

At the same time as that I approached *Rough
Guide*. I found out they were looking for people to
suggest titles. So I suggested a few, heard nothing
back for four months then suddenly got this email
saying, 'do you want to meet for lunch to discuss
things?' So I was like, 'okay, yeah sure,' so I ended
up getting treated to a nice cannelloni [laughs]
at this restaurant and this guy, Andrew Lockett,
was saying he liked the titles I'd suggested, in
particular the brain. Oh, okay I thought, then
three quarters of the way through the meal he just
said, 'would you do it?' and it was just this really
weird moment where I found myself saying yes to
it without fully grasping the implications of what
I'd just agreed to.

I went home and told Charmaine and she asked
how much it was going to pay, and I didn't have
a bloody clue! So that was it basically for a year,
which sounds like a long time but that was an
incredibly intense period, I think there was
about eleven or twelve chapters, so I had to do
about three weeks of research followed by an
intense week of writing per chapter. So, when
you're trying to make your approach on say
consciousness, you have to think, erm right, what's
known about consciousness and then you have to
try and distil it down so that normal people, like
myself and my parents, can grasp it and it was

quite a big task. So that kind of took away from the film-making but it was a really good thing to do and a really nice thing to happen.

With the film-making I realised that I wanted to get back into that and to do so I had to really, really extend my network. I sought out competitions and opportunities and made the most of them. For instance, Channel 4 had an online thing, BT had an online film thing too, so I was constantly making my little mash-ups and sending them in to see if anyone would take notice, and they did which was incredibly gratifying. But the big thing and the most relevant breakthrough was when Sheffield Documentary Film Festival was holding a competition and I just submitted a pitch for this film I wanted to make about drugs and I managed to get shortlisted for that competition. I went up there and sitting amongst a bunch of about ten people and we essentially did our pitches. Afterwards this producer came up to me - Andy Glynn - and he said, 'why don't you come and have a chat some time?'

I ended up going to see Andy and developing a series of pitches for *Three Minute Wonder* for Channel 4 which allowed me to make four broadcast documentaries all about an area I loved, which was neuroscience. That was quite a lovely breakthrough - not only because it was on broadcast TV; I didn't *really* care that much about that, but it was more about the learning; it enabled me to work with professional editors. I was making my version of a film having shot it and they would then continue to refine it and that was an incredibly interesting process and I learnt an awful lot about editing when I worked with those people.

The next big thing was, again seeking out these opportunities, I went to something called Crossover, which is a five day long residential experience where you've got to collaborate with architects, game designers, programmers and just basically come up with ideas that you then pitch at the end of the week. That was a really interesting experience and again I met people there, who then recommended me for a project called Routes. The weird thing about that was I got this invitation to go and meet these people for lunch. I was sitting down and talking to them and the whole time thinking they were asking me to be an assistant camera on this documentary they were making. I was like 'okay'. It was my understanding at the time that there would be someone else running the show, directing it, editing and stuff like that and I was really there for pick-up shots and to get other things. Towards the end of the meeting, I asked if they could just recap on that and they were like, 'no, no, we don't want you to be the assistant camera, we want you to shoot and edit all eight episodes of the series we're doing'. I was like 'Ahhhh' [laughs] because I did not feel ready for that. This was a project that was going on between Channel 4 and the Wellcome Trust, who I was aware of because they'd funded me when I was a scientist but it felt like a really big project. I was quite nervous about it. Anyway I remember the day before filming for the first time being absolutely terrified and I really had to get a grip! I went and met Katherine Ryan, the comedian. I was filming at her flat and out walking the dog and stuff like that and we just had a laugh and she was brilliant and I cobbled together a rough fifteen minute edit to show the people from Channel 4 and they were like, 'yup, this is the stuff we want'. After that I basically went out, did a lot more filming for them, edited it and it went on to be this project Routes, which was this lovely, huge online fusion of documentary and gaming and it was just a brilliant project to be in and that was the stepping stone to get me into Wellcome. Because they had worked with me and they could see what I did when a job became available I applied for it.

ME: That was very interesting...

BG: Thank you [laughs].

ME: Thanks Barry, that was interesting... So in terms of advice, what would you tell people looking at pursuing their dreams? You've pursued, with great success, two distinct fields: what do you put that down to? Good fortune? Or is it hard work and making yourself available, networking? What's the magic bullet?

BG: Yeah I think it's being, there's always luck involved, but I think you have to be pure to what drives you and what interests you. So for a period of my life I was really interested in scientific pursuits, scientific questions, but then I became aware of the emerging creative desires which I then decided to pursue and I think it's a combination of tenacity and purity of will to think to yourself, 'if I am, suddenly, going to try and become this thing, like a film-maker, what do I have to do?' And so you kind of immerse yourself in the culture, find out what you need to know, mix with other film-makers, go to where they are going and really just basically chameleonise yourself - you just become one.

At the beginning you feel like you're faking it; it's taken me a long time actually to get away from that sense that you're just faking it, that you're an imposter. But then after long enough, you realise you are, I am a film-maker, and you've somehow got from there to there. But it did involve being open to opportunity, it did involve recognising that you have to get out there with the camera. I get a lot of people who write to me saying, 'oh I'd really like to be a film-maker' and I'm like 'yeah, I know, a lot of people do, so go and be one'. It's kind of harsh in a way, but you have to try it and discover for yourself whether you really do want to be a film-maker because not everyone takes to the combined act of production and filming and editing and doing a bit of post-production and then fiddling around with it on-line to try and get it views and stuff like that. But then, if you want to be taken seriously by people that you might want to get a job from, they need to have something to see, they need to get a sense of what your flair is, what your style is, because ultimately your films become a reflection of who you are as a person.

For me, I've discovered that I'm some kind of weird poetic, science thing that just loves trying to make thoughtful films about science that touch on the nature of what it means to be human and all this stuff that sounds really wanky when you say it out loud. It really is important to get something made; that would be the bottom line. Don't keep talking about it, drill into the kind of thing you'd like to make and then have a crack at it, even if it's complete crap - it will be, stuff I made was complete crap - but all the time you're making things that are not great you are learning how to use the camera equipment, the editing software, you are getting better.

ME: Yeah, it's the same reason that no one announces they want to be a surgeon and people just taking it on faith that you can do this?

BG: Yeah [laughs].

ME: Do you think there's going to be a Phase 3? You're still a relatively young man [laughs]. Is there something different on the horizon for you?

BG: That's a really good question. Maybe. But I'm not sure what it is yet, there's an itch but I'm not quite sure how to scratch it at the moment, but I can feel something. I guess I'd do what I usually do which is get interested in something, start thinking about it more than what I am currently doing, resign and then go off and try and make a living out of it [laughs].

ME: Looking back at the decisions you've made, do you consider it to be brave or foolish?

BG: At the time it never felt brave; at the time it felt absolutely necessary. A lot of people told me it was brave but I think the only thing, when people say that, they're just talking about money. I think as long as you're able to somehow financially support yourself then I don't think it matters as long as you're happy in what you're doing.

ME: Thank you.

5

ARE YOU EXPERIENCED?

'Experience is one thing you can't
get for nothing.'
Oscar Wilde

I ronically many of you won't even know what the chapter title refers to; that's experience for you (it's Jimi Hendrix by the way) and although it's irrelevant here it does help clarify what I mean by experience in this context. Experience here is less to do with age and how many times you've been around the block but rather the value of the activities you've taken part in, the situations you've put yourself in and what you've learnt from them. Doing something without learning from it can't reasonably be considered an experience - it's just something you did - but an admissions tutor, an employer, someone who can offer you help and guidance, wants to understand the how and why of your journey, what you've learnt along the way, how that knowledge and experience has benefitted you and how it informs what/how you do things and what you hope to learn as you continue.

As Wilde says at the top of the page, 'Experience is one thing you can't get for nothing'; indeed he may even have been selling it short as you could also possibly get paid.

Is work experience good?

Dumb question, right? Evidently, it's good, but it's good in ways you may not even have considered yet. Unfortunately it's not usually done well which somewhat damages the point of it. Most students I've worked with or spoken to have had some form of work experience placement organised by their school. A laudable and noble aim but the vast majority of students tend to have a rubbish time of it, most of them seemed to either work in an uncle's office doing photocopying, or in a primary school that their school had links to. Those are just two examples and may not reflect what happened/happens in your school, but overwhelmingly with the people I've dealt with, the placements didn't speak to what they wanted to do or reflect where they wanted to go.

How do we change that?

Simply put, you need to get off your butts. The school can only ever do so much - remember this is your life, not theirs; if they've got to organise work for 150 kids some of you are going to slip through the net. If they were a lifeguard and you were drowning along with another 149 kids you'd probably give swimming a shot rather than bobbing up and down in the water. Take charge of your own life and sort out work experience that is relevant and interesting for you. Plus, businesses and people will respond much more favourably to someone with a genuine interest and passion for a subject who has the chops to come and ask for help rather than having a disinterested teenager being foisted upon them.

What do I get from it?

As we touched on earlier, making a decision in a vacuum is never a good idea. The choices you make, a bit like science, should be weighed using all the available evidence, not simply best guesses and random finger-pointing. Yes you can start with a hypothesis but it should be one that you stress-test and push and question and second guess. If, as we discussed before, you decide you want a career in the law, it is at the stage of inception nothing more than an idea, an idea based on any number of factors but none of them will be rooted in practical and demonstrable reality. The only way to understand what being a lawyer may actually entail, from the culture to the reality of the work, is to be in an environment where law is practised. We've all seen legal dramas on TV and film, but in the UK at least (and quite likely the US) it's probably a lot more paperwork-heavy and considerably less exciting. By going to do some work experience you achieve several key goals:

- You gain genuine first-hand experience of the normal working life of someone in that area.

- You have the opportunity to ask professionals already doing what you want to do about not just the reality of the job, but how they got there, and what they did that helped them get started.

- You begin to build your professional network. These people, if you perform well and are articulate, professional and show enthusiasm, may give you additional work experience whilst you're studying.

- The people you meet may also offer you letters of recommendation or warm introductions to other professionals who may be able to help.

These are just some of the invaluable benefits available to you. Additionally you can learn more about yourself and your own preferences:

- You may discover something about the working culture/reality of the job that makes you drastically rethink your options. This may be initially discouraging but it's much better to find out now than after a three year degree.

- It may help you refine precisely what area you may wish to go into, for example you may discover that working in a high street solicitors isn't quite right for you and you'd rather work in a corporate environment within finance or insurance or do legal work for a larger business.

- Being in a professional environment might help inform how you think of yourself, give you a clearer view of the kind of person you need to be to fit into that environment and what kind of soft skills you should develop to thrive.

- You will become accustomed to speaking with adults in a businesslike manner, telling your story, selling yourself, gaining a raft of professional comportment skills that will make you considerably more comfortable in an interview situation in the future.

By doing more and more work experience you continue to build a professional network of people that may be inclined to and be able to help you progress in your career. You also have an impressive track record that you can now present to an admissions tutor or potential employer to demonstrate your long-standing commitment to and interest in your chosen field.

For all of the above reasons, and I'm certain many more, this is why quality (note the key word here - quality) work experience is so important and not just a box-ticking chore to get off your plate. There's no excuse for any of you to not be doing this. No matter what your background or circumstances, if you can pick up a phone or look on the internet you can find a business that does what you want and you can call them. You all have a holiday about every seven weeks, you finish school or college around half three; all of this time could be used to do little bits of work: a half day here and there over the course of a couple of years adds up.

How do I organise it?

Same message as before, get off your butt and do it! The shiny-things obsessed brain worm will find a way to encourage you to put it off, procrastinate, and otherwise derail your best intentions, but you need to just get on and do it. But how to begin?

- Identify the areas in which you are interested. This could be a variety of things - remember half the point of this exercise is to prove or disprove your interest in a certain area. If you're not sure, give it a whirl, stick it on the list. A couple of hours out of your life is hardly going to derail the whole process and you might surprise yourself positively or negatively - either way it's all good because you've learned a little something.

- Get on the internet, look at local companies that are working in this area, look at their websites; the more you know about them the more you can refine who you approach and explain to them what specifically about them interests you.

- Ask your parents and parents' friends and friends' parents who they know. Is there anyone in your extended network that may be able to help you? Don't be afraid to ask - they can only say no.

- Make a list of the companies most suited to what you want to explore.

- Develop a short sales pitch/rehearse what you want to say when you introduce yourself.

- Get on the phone, go to their offices, send them an email and make sure that your email address is work-appropriate, no 'BigBoi69's or 'Sexylegs' please. No one thinks it's funny.

- That's it!

When you break it down like that it's really not so very hard is it? Have a think, make some calls. Simple. Yet most people don't do this anywhere near enough, if at all.

What do I say? How do I ask?

There are two important things to remember here - don't try and be clever, and get to the point. People, generally speaking, are good eggs and will happily give you some of their time, but they owe you nothing, so do your research, be prepared and don't waste their valuable time. You are entering their world, not they yours, so act accordingly - be professional, sincere, courteous and grateful.

Broadly speaking there will be three forms of approach - phone or email or turning up. Turning up is a pretty ballsy move as it pretty much demands an instant reaction; they may be impressed or if they're busy or having a bad day it could push them over the edge. But with a CV and a winning smile the receptionist may take pity on you and give your details to the person you need. Otherwise it probably begins with calling their reception and asking who it is you need to speak to. Don't overcomplicate it but do prepare in advance so you know what you are asking.

A simple example would be something like this:

> 'Hi there. I was hoping you may be able to help. My name is X., I'm a student at X. I'm thinking about pursuing a career in X and was wondering whether there was anyone in the business I could speak to about coming in to do some work experience just to get a sense of what it's actually like?'

In all likelihood whoever answers the phone may say one of three things -

- That's not really something we do.

- Yes, that will be Bob you need to speak to. Let me see if he's available. (Other names may be available.)

- Yes, the person you need to speak to is Colin (see?) I can give you his email address.

You should deal with any of these with grace and courtesy - rejection is a big part of life and work, so you mustn't take it too personally. If you've spent ages steeling yourself to make that first call and you get shot down it can really wind you. Don't be put off; it's not you. How could it be? You said three sentences; sometimes companies just don't do it. The next one may. If they put you straight through just remain calm; if you've done your preparation you should be just fine. The important thing to remember is that you may have to answer questions, they will likely ask things like:

- What is it you want to do?

- What about this career interests you?

- What do you want to learn?

- What do you think we can teach you/show you?

- What are you hoping to get out of this?

- When are you available to come in?

It's important that you have thought about these things in advance and have rehearsed at least a few responses. As I said earlier, they are giving up their time: don't waste it by saying 'erm' and 'I dunno, stuff and that'. Think about your objectives and be honest with them, don't try and dress it up; people respond to honesty - they don't expect you to be a polished professional with answers to everything but they will expect you to try to behave accordingly and at least have an idea about what your objectives are. How can they help you if you don't even know what you want?

The final option is that you will be given an email address and a contact name and, much like with your initial pitch to the reception, you drop them an email explaining who you are and why you are emailing them. In this scenario don't pester them, give them at least a week to come back before following up, at which point call reception again and explain the situation, asking if you could speak to them. If they don't respond, don't push the matter; sometimes life gets in the way. Ideally you will have a number of other approaches live at the same time so your eggs should be in lots of baskets.

What do I need to do next?

Like so many things in life it comes down to research and preparation - the more you learn about a business through their website, online articles, trade papers etc, the better quality questions you can ask. The better quality questions you can ask, the more impressed the people will be: it shows commitment and dedication and they will respond in kind by being more invested in helping you if you show how much you care and that you are passionate about what they do.

Think about what you want to get from it. This is the crucial part of the equation and is massively linked to the preparation you'll have done. Don't waste your or their time by asking questions that are already answered on their website or elsewhere. Think about the bits of information they are sitting on that you couldn't learn elsewhere - now, that could be anything from 'how did they get into X job?' to 'could I sit in on X?' The point is you're there to learn, to educate yourself, not just to take up room for an afternoon. So, if you're particularly interested in a certain thing they do but want to see that thing done first-hand - to either sense-check that the reality lives up to your imagined version of it, or because you want to get involved simply so you've first-hand experience of it – then ask. They can only tell you 'no,' but likelier than not they'll be impressed that you've done your research and clearly have an idea of what they do and where you want to be. The more research you can do in advance the better quality questions you can ask.

What do I do when I'm there?

As we touched on in the previous section, what to do when you're there is the difference between having a valuable experience and making useful contacts or spending a half day following a stranger around their workplace.

FIRSTLY - Dress for the occasion. We'll get into this more in a later chapter but appearances do matter. Don't try and be something you're not by wearing your Dad's suit or your Mum's pearls but do make an effort. Clean, ironed shirt, tie, pressed trousers and shined shoes or equivalent - unless you're looking for work at a fashion house, you're not there to make a statement about your individuality. You're never going to upset someone by being slightly overdressed but they will remember you for all the wrong reasons if you dress badly. Also, wash your hair and if it's long tie it back. Cut your fingernails, shave whatever you need to. You may feel the need to rail against this because of youthful non-conformity, but the only form of non-conformity is conforming to non-conformity. I know this because once upon a time I had long hair and spent most of my life trying to adopt an air of being an unimpressed, joyless genius for whom the tedium of simply being alive was sometimes all too much. And I used to wear ladies' blouses from the 70s that I found in the school wardrobe department. In the end it all got to be rather too much trouble and, equipped with the knowledge that at some point you'll probably bow to conformity, for the sake of making a good impression just scrub up.

SECONDLY - Behave accordingly: this is a place of business, this is people's reality. This is how they make their money. Be mindful of the fact that whoever you're dealing with or meeting on the day is giving up their time for no reason other than to help you; you are there at the indulgence of the staff and managers, so be gracious, courteous and respectful. That means speaking when spoken to, firm handshakes, eye contact, knowing when to speak and when to listen, relying on your research to answer any questions/ask any questions as and when appropriate. Basically behave as if you're meeting your boyfriend or girlfriend's parents for the first time.

THIRDLY - Offer to help, get stuck in, ask questions. Really make the most of the experience. Of course the more you get stuck in the more you'll get out of it but perhaps more crucially you might leave a good enough impression with the company that you could get more work experience out of them in the future, in your holidays, half terms etc, and get a letter of recommendation or similar. How much you get from these first forays into the professional marketplace and how lasting their impact may be is entirely down to you and the effort you are willing to put in. You've come this far so don't half arse it now.

Don't ask too much and don't take the mickey

As I've tried to underline throughout the chapter, people are generally pretty generous with their time if they believe that the person asking something of them is sincere and committed to the process - your half of the deal is to understand that and recognise they are doing you a favour, for no other reason than they are being nice. Don't rearrange it unless you have a very strong reason to do so, don't make unreasonable demands on their time or ask too much of them in terms of their having to handle you, be punctual - ten minutes early is better than one minute late - do your homework.

Conclusion

The best quality work experience provides you with a raft of benefits that you probably hadn't considered as your teacher was telling you that you ought to do some. These benefits are as follows:

- Confirms or denies your interest in a field.

- Refines and hones your interest in a field.

- Refines and hones your preferences regarding working culture, with people, on your own etc.

- Makes you sell yourself, your interest.

- Develops professional comportment skills.

- Makes you talk on a level with adults in a professional setting, useful for interviews amongst other things.

- Builds your understanding of a field and career path.

- Unparalleled access to real world, first-hand accounts of how to succeed in the profession and the reality of working in it.

- Helps you develop your research and application skills.

- Adds to your developing portfolio of experiences that can add weight to a personal statement or CV.

- Begins to build your professional network.

- Can forge links that may be useful for ongoing work experience, internships etc.

- Can yield letters of recommendation and exposure to the people you met's wider network.

So, when your school tells you that you should be doing this, you should be telling them you already have. This is such a crucial element of the academic and careers pathway that it's impossible to overstate it. Too often during the process of schooling this is done in the summer term of your first year of A levels, after which you go on holiday and then when you're back you have a couple of months to make your decision and do all your planning and write a personal statement. You should be doing this from fifteen onwards: the more time you have, the more convincing a portfolio of activities you have to present to an employer, an apprenticeship or an admissions tutor. What if the thing you thought you always wanted to do turned out to be horrible and you have to reassess everything in a matter of months? Doesn't it just make sense to find out as early as possible? By doing this, and doing it well, it makes choices regarding course selection (if you're university bound) or identifying a career path a hundred times easier - logically it follows that if you don't know what career you want to head towards, choosing a degree or further training is an almost impossible task but if you know exactly what you want to do, it's a doddle.

CASE STUDY

SARAH ANN KENNEDY

The incomparable sardonic voice of Nanny Plum in Ben & Holly's Little Kingdom, the multi-talented Miss Rabbit in Peppa Pig and Royal College trained artist, animator and show runner, now lecturing at UCLAN, Sarah Ann Kennedy divides her time between being very serious and helping students fulfil their professional ambitions and making pre-schoolers everywhere laugh.

ME: Could you just give me a bit of background on your professional and academic life and how you got from where you started to where you are now?

SK: Right, gosh, that's quite a long story. Basically I was quite naughty at school. I liked doing art but was advised quite strongly against because they said that I would never get a job as an artist so I did it as an extra subject when I was doing my A levels. I did all the wrong A levels: Physics, Maths and Biology, which of course I hated. I didn't even want to open a book and in the end I failed them all. In the meantime, I had been drawing in my room, so rather than do my maths homework, I literally just drew, so I had this great portfolio of work. When I failed everything my mum was at the end of her tether with me. I had a summer job working in a factory, packing car components, parts for cars, and she got in a right old panic that I was going to end up there - and, to be fair, so did I. I went for an interview for an art foundation course about a week before the course started, and I was accepted on the course. I arrived and once the course started I thought, 'I've come home, I really love this and why on earth didn't I do this before?'

Once on the foundation, a whole world opened up to me. Suddenly I realised that my art education at school had been quite limited: drawing, observational drawing and painting. Suddenly you could do jewellery, textiles, furniture, you could do theatre design, you could do film design, you know, on a foundation course you do everything. There are so many things you are introduced to and it was really exciting. This whole world of options and careers and jobs opened up although I didn't at that point think about animation; it was very fine art focused so I basically ended up doing fine art. What I liked about it was that you could talk about ideas and that's what I found exciting. At that time, you didn't have modules in education you just went and did your degree and got a mark at the end of the year. So in fine art, I made the choice to go to Newcastle and you just had a space and did your own work and you had to give seminars to show what you were doing.

All my cohort ended up doing incredibly well. One of them has been nominated for the Turner Prize, another's Head of Painting at the RCA (Royal College of Art) and is now running this big gallery in New York. At the time I didn't realise I was going to quite a good place until I realised I was slightly more frightened of my cohorts' reaction rather than that of my tutors. We'd give a seminar and everyone would attack you and you would have to explain yourself, so it really lifted the standard of work. At the end of that I thought, oh my God, what am I going to do? I did some installation, I took loads of photographs and I had made some animated films on the course as well because it was easier than trying to get a crew together. I did everything myself. I wrote them, literally had no idea what I was doing but I wrote all the stories, created all the characters, did the voices and made the sets. I had a little Bolex camera that I wound up and then would animate frame by frame. I would sit in there for hours. I didn't want a great big camera that other people were using to make fine art films, so I had this little crappy camera but actually it was great; it meant I could just get on with stuff.

When I got to my third year I applied to the Royal College and I got in amazingly. What I liked about it was that I quite liked performing, I liked drama, I liked drawing. It just encompassed everything I enjoyed. I liked telling stories and it was all about character so I felt that was where I wanted to be. When I was at the RCA I learned how to actually make a film. I had literally no idea, I didn't even know you were supposed to make storyboards, or do character design; before I had just got on with it. So when I sold my first year film to Channel 4 I was really amazed. Everyone else there had been doing animation courses, and I felt they were all much better; I was like a feral student. I made this first year film called 'Honestly this is the story of my life'. It was a set project about our lives. I created a story about a girl who didn't really fit; she was a bit lost on her course and didn't know what to do so just wandered around London thinking about what to do and in the end didn't really do anything. It was all about that lack of confidence and learning about London and being slightly self-conscious about having an A-Z and

not knowing anything. It was all about that kind
of stuff, and it's just been re-bought by the BFI
and they are going to redistribute it, which is
quite exciting because I haven't seen it for years
as it's on 16mm film.

Then I had my final year and everyone said
if you don't get a job when you're at the Royal
College degree show then you'll never work in the
industry. Of course I didn't get a job at the degree
show and I thought, 'that's it, my life is over.,
What am I going to do?' I spent six months being
quite depressed but I did manage to get a job at
the Royal Court Theatre, working in the bookshop
at the theatre three days a week and I thought I'd
do writing for the other two. I actually found
they treated me quite badly although to be honest
I didn't really know what I was doing. I felt quite
low at this point but I think everyone is when
they leave uni. When you suddenly go into the
world it's quite a shock, because everything's been
mapped out until that point and then suddenly
you're in this huge place.

Even though I'd sold this film I was quite lost
and all of my friends seemed to be getting quite
technical jobs. I'd worked for companies during
my time at the RCA on films like *Who Framed
Roger Rabbit?* Also I started the sound breakdown
for this other thing called *Muzzy* so I had done
quite a lot of stuff.

ME: Sorry, what was the other thing?

SK: It was a thing the BBC did for teaching languages
to kids. I've noticed they've started re-selling
it. My tutor made it so I worked for him one

summer doing all the sound. You have to break the sound down phonetically, so I did that and then I worked on *Roger Rabbit* one Easter, painting mattes so I had working experience. Then Channel 4 phoned me up and said, 'Oh your film, we really like it. Do you want to do the title sequence for this production company?' I thought I'd be a bit out of my depth so I went to see them and I wasn't sure whether I wanted to do it or not and then I came up with another idea to do something else for them. A little short thing called *Family Favourites*, which was a film about how hard Christmas can be. It wasn't all jolly, instead everything was a nightmare, just a funny little cartoon. Then I got a job as a researcher working for them. I did that for six months and when I was there I started pitching an idea for a series called *Nights* to the commissioning editor, a guy called Stephen Garrett (Executive Producer for *Spooks* and *The Night Manager*). At that point he didn't commission it; he was interested, he read the script but then I got a job on *Eastenders* because my contract had finished for that series. Then I worked for *Eastenders* for six months, where I learned loads. I hated it, I really hated it but I learned a lot in terms of story structure, character biogs, synopsis and all that stuff I really didn't know much about.

I kept hassling Stephen Garrett at Channel 4 until he finally commissioned me to make a one-off ten minute short called *Nights* as part of a new writer/talent showcase. I made that and then I took a risk. I left a staff job at the BBC, which were quite hard to come by, but I just wasn't very good at working in the factory system. I found I just wasn't quite ready for that kind of life. I just wanted to do a bit more of my own stuff and from that I put in a proposal for a series of *Nights* which got commissioned. I rented the stop frame studio at *Spitting Image* - there weren't many people doing stop motion and this was one of the only studios in London. Then I got to know the guys at *Spitting Image* and in particularly Roger Law (creator of *Spitting Image*). He said, 'you should come and work here' and I said, 'okay but I want to do my own stuff' so he asked me to come up with an idea and I came up with *Crapston Villas*. I'd tried to get it off the ground elsewhere but it didn't work so I told him about it and asked if we could do it. He said yes so I developed it with them and then after I finished *Nights*, I began *Crapston Villas*, which was an animated soap. Because I'd worked on *Eastenders* I understood how to structure it all properly, like the cliff-hangers and intertwining storylines.

In the meantime, my friend Candy, for whom I always did voices, got her own series commissioned and I played Dolly, the main character. I met Candy at Newcastle. We both did animations in our own maverick weird way and we also wrote a play together and took it to the Edinburgh Festival in between our second and third year. Anyway, she got this series called *Pond Life* off the ground about the same time as I was doing *Crapston*, so I was really busy with the voices for *Pond Life* as well as writing and directing *Crapston*.

After series one I went to Africa to see my brother and had a really bad accident. When I came home I lay on my back writing the second

series but I was in terrible pain and told them I
couldn't direct it. They had to get someone else
whilst I was recovering and I suddenly thought,
I have enough money in my bank to pay my
mortgage but I haven't got any sick pay and I did
the PPI thing but they wouldn't pay it and they
wouldn't pay the mortgage. I had no security and
it made me decide I need to change my life 'cause
actually I could be ill again. I had about two years
doing voice-over work and trying different things
and wondering what I should do that's not such
hard work and will give me more security.

I retrained and got into education and that's when
I became a lecturer but I carried on doing a little
bit of voice-over work and some writing 'cause
I liked it and that's when I met Mark and Nev
[Mark Baker and Neville Astley - creators of *Peppa
Pig*]. *Crapston* was so rude with so much swearing
I thought, 'who's going to give me a job in kids?'
BBC and Channel 4 had stopped commissioning
adults' stuff so I wasn't sure what I was going to
do. Mark and Nev had a similar problem but came
up with this fabulous idea for *Peppa Pig*. We
were sharing a studio then and they were quite
sweet and they asked me, 'do you know any writers
that might like to do a bit of writing on *Peppa*?
We've got it off the ground?' I was like, 'I dunno,
I'll have a bit of a think,' and then they said,
'well actually we mean you.' and I couldn't believe
it. 'Me?' I couldn't believe it. I wrote a couple of
episodes and then there was a character that was
working in a shop and that was Miss Rabbit. The
character just grew and grew. I went off to work
in education and they kept writing more of this
stuff, which is fabulous, and then they wrote *Ben
and Holly* and wrote Nanny Plum for me.

ME: I genuinely love *Ben and Holly.* I have a seven and a four year old and even though they're probably too old for it now they keep putting it on in their room and I can just hear laughter coming down the stairs.

SK: Ahhh, that's good - it's really popular. I saw this thing on Facebook and it was voted number one most popular children's series. *Ben & Holly* was number one and *Peppa* was number two. It was kind of an accident that I got into that. A very lucky accident. The main thing for me was that I always just followed my heart so whatever I found I liked doing and I was quite good at, that's the thing I tried to concentrate on rather than trying to force myself into something that I wasn't. I think I learned that lesson early on.

The main thing for me is that I just wanted to do things that make me feel happy really. I really like teaching, I really love animation and I like what you can do with it and I like showing the students the things they haven't seen and going through the process with them. I like it when they get a buzz and love what they're doing. Because of my industry contacts - I worked in industry for quite a few years before going into education, and still do - it helps me stay up to date with everything. I can advise them about which software to use, what's going on. I go to lots of things, I stay in touch with lots of people and it helps the students when they leave as I try to really prepare them for the world. I remember my fear, even though I'd been reasonably well prepared, I remember that sudden, terrible fear that Soho seemed such a massive place and I thought I don't even know where to start. Whereas I get them to do searches on what's in this area, who they can speak to, how did they put the show together, who's the producer. It's a key part of the course, putting together an action plan on how they are going to go out and approach the world. I would always advise them to just get in, get in there, it doesn't matter what you are doing, get in there and meet them, pitch them ideas or you can kind of show them other things you can do. Basically most people just want to work with people they like. That's the reality. So if you're nice and quite keen and you've got some talent you'll do alright.

ME: The fact that you are thinking beyond university is not necessarily standard practice. I know a lot of people feel quite abandoned once their studies are out of the way. How important to you is it for school leavers or university students to have that kind of through vision? With you it doesn't sound like you had a cast-iron plan when you set off on your journey but it sounds like you think it's quite a good thing now. What sort of level of importance do you attach to having a solid plan if you were advising people now?

SK: I think when I was on foundation I remember saying to a tutor - this was when Channel 4 had literally just started - that my sister and I would have a comedy show and you just book slots; I had no idea what I was talking about and in the end I did sort of do that! I wanted to do my own stuff, but you have to have realistic goals. I say to the students, everybody wants to be either a director or a producer but you have to be really realistic. Is that actually what you like or are you good at, or are you good at some other aspect of that? Be honest with yourself about what it is you feel you can do and don't expect to do it as soon as you leave. There isn't a set path with any of the creative industries; there's always a kind of weird route that you go round to get to it. So have a long aim, and that can change, you don't have to stick to it, that can change as you go along but then have lots of smaller, achievable goals along the way and that builds your confidence.

I think that's the thing: if you aim too high too soon, you get really depressed 'cause you get knocked back all the time. I've had students say to me, 'I'm going to go and work for Pixar', but how? You're not experienced enough, you need to start with something small. You might think, eventually I want to work there. I had one student on the MA and he works for this massive animation company and he's done really well, but he was really realistic. He said, 'I want to work on an award-winning film' and I said, 'I'm sure you will one day if you want to do that.' He worked really hard on the MA and then I put him in touch with some people in Canada that I knew from years ago at Channel 4. He and his wife had emigrated, he was a mature student, sorted all that out. But he was really realistic and he just got any job in Vancouver to start with so I put him in touch with these people and said, 'he doesn't know anyone but he loves animation' and he was a nice bloke and he made friends with them and he got a job as a production assistant working for this quite big animation company.

Later he told them he had this MA, and he showed them his work, and they were like, why are you working on this? You need to be doing this, and now he's working as an animator, working his way up - but he did it by taking realistic steps and then you go on to get a job at Pixar.

But otherwise as soon as they don't get a job
at Pixar they're depressed. You just need to be
really, really realistic about how to get to where
you want to be. You need to move to where the
opportunities are, seek out where to go, what
to do, be realistic about the standard of your
work; what do you need to learn? If you've not
demonstrated certain skills you're going to be hard
pressed to get a job on a series. The earlier you
start to think about these things the easier it will
be to get to where you want to.

ME: That echoes a lot of what I've said in this book
- the need to set small, achievable goals and to
be honest about what you can and can't do. The
other question - it feels kind of crass to even ask,
as you're the only person I've interviewed that
I would ask this question of - as a mother and a
woman finding that work-life balance seems to be
a consideration that is more acute than it is for
many men. What sort of advice would you offer to
young women coming through now?

SK: It's not crass at all. Aanimation is an industry
that expects you to dedicate a lot of your life if
you want to be successful at it. When I was single,
which was most of my 'working' career other than
intermittent relationships, it was fine, but I
never really had time for anything else. I had
children much later, in my forties. I was lucky
because many can't. I met my husband older and
my life was very different. We live much longer
and you can have different careers within your
life, you can have a career up until you're forty
and then another from forty until whenever. I
think my life changed quite a lot, for a variety of
reasons. People can manage it and I think things

aren't so strict now. You just have to be flexible. If you have to be around your kids more then you can seek out other areas within your field that are maybe less restrictive. There are times when you need to focus on your career and there are times when you need to focus on your family; you just have to set your boundaries. I don't think women should be put off trying to forge a career because if you're in the right relationship you'll find a way to make it work.

ME: You've a daughter haven't you?

SK: Yes, I've got a little girl. Well, she's eight now.

ME: Have your experiences in industry, particularly such a male-dominated one as the media, informed how and what you would tell her to do?

SK: When I first started working I wanted an all-female crew for *Crapston Villas* but they just weren't there so I worked with all blokes and although they never said anything you could see them giving looks and stuff and it was upsetting. So I would go outside and have a cry, and come back in and be like, 'Hi!' I just didn't want to be 'the hysterical woman'. In the end it was brilliant and we all loved working on it though, but it was hard turning that around. It was like I had to be extra good to get the same level of respect.

ME: Are you quite gung-ho when it comes to encouraging your daughter's ambitions?

SK: Yeah, she sees me working hard and I just say, do what you want. She's aware of it though and sometimes says, 'well that's not fair' and I explain that in those days boys did that more than girls, but it's not like that now and you just go for what you want. I don't go on and on about it; I just don't give her limits. I just focus on what she likes doing and I try and encourage that. She's only little but she wants to be a vet so she watches loads of animal programmes and I tell her she'll have to work hard and she just says, okay. She also wants to live in a bungalow in London.

ME: Well you can't move for bungalows in London.

SK: That's her plan. I say to her everything achievable.

ME: What advice would you give to young people generally, coming through at fifteen, sixteen, seventeen, regardless of their background?

SK: Follow your heart. Sometimes you like the idea of being something and that can be different to what you like doing. Usually you're quite good at what you like doing, so it might be something really unusual, so you might be really good at maths or art or whatever so follow that, because you'll find a path and you'll try harder because you enjoy it. Whatever you do, it is a competitive world so if you're struggling a bit with something, I'm not saying give up at the first hurdle but some things you find easier than others and if you do, you'll make the effort to work through those tough, difficult bits. If it's difficult already it's more of a struggle, so go for the things you like doing and you'll find a career doing it.

ME: Thank you very much.

6

NO STUPID QUESTIONS

'There is no stupid question. Stupid
people don't ask questions.'

Unknown

'Everybody's a genius. But if you judge a fish by
its ability to climb a tree, it will live its whole
life believing that it is stupid.'

Albert Einstein (attributed)

In this chapter we are going to look at a range of techniques and good practice behaviours you could, and should, be adopting to help you ask the right questions of the right people and find out everything you need and want to know.

It almost goes without saying that you can't know everything, but, worryingly, most of us don't even know to recognise that we don't know what we don't yet know. There's no expectation on you at this stage to be the finished, polished and highly buffed article, and now more than ever you can and should be asking as many questions as you possibly can. About everything. I do mean everything - politics, religion, economics, types of job, foreign policy, what you call those little plastic bits on the ends of laces (flugelbinder or aglet), be curious about the world around you and the more you ask the better informed you can be. It's important for so many reasons beyond general preparedness, but crucially for this too, if you have a context by which to understand the world around you it could very well shape the part you want to play in it.

All of you are by now, I'm quite sure, pretty adept with how to look things up, get quick answers to questions you may have. But to truly understand an issue or an area that you are interested in you need to go beyond scratching the surface of it by looking at Wikipedia. This is important regardless of where your path may take you. An admissions tutor looking at a personal statement or potentially interviewing you wants to see passion, of course, but also depth of understanding, informed, well thought through arguments and opinions which are not based on a quick squizz at an article or two, but a demonstrable and consistent devotion to a subject. This is just as necessary if applying for an apprenticeship or a job. People need to see that you are taking this as seriously as they do and being well informed helps sell that narrative.

There are a number of tools in your toolkit for this kind of thing and we're going to work our way through them together.

Internet based research.

Using your extended network.

Work experience.

Informational interviewing.

Newspapers and trade magazines.

Related societies and associations.

I recognise that saying 'ask questions' may be a little vague so, in the interest of linking this to a real world example and to show the application of these tips in a meaningful way, we're going to pretend that you want to become an accountant. What do I look into? What do I need to find out? What do I not know that I don't know?

Internet based research

This is the lowest hanging fruit and the easiest to do bits of on an 'as and when' basis. On the bus to school or college, hop onto Google and get some answers. This is by far the most effective tool you have in your toolkit; it's saturation bombing rather than a sniper rifle. Yes, you will come across a lot of stuff that is irrelevant to you, but you can whittle it down. Start with the basics - how to become an accountant? You will quickly learn there are a number of different routes and qualifications you can work towards depending on what kind of accountant you want to be. A degree, whilst not necessary, could certainly be advantageous - something like business and accountancy would be a solid bedrock, but equally with no prior qualifications you could work towards your AAT (Association of Accounting Technicians). You could enjoy a solid career with just this qualification but there are further levels available that will broaden your options and deepen your experience such as CIMA (Chartered Institute of Management Accountants) or ACCA (Association of Chartered Certified Accountants). Once you've established this you can start to explore the length of time and cost of doing each of these qualifications. Look at big firms that may support you through your qualifications. What do they look for? What are their requirements? Identify any trends in the market at the moment: Is there a shortage of a particular type of accountant? Where could the job take you? Do you want to work for an accountancy firm or work in-house for a large Public limited company, maybe a law firm? Do you want to move towards being a Financial Director and then ultimately a Managing Director of a business? All of these questions and the different routes are fairly easily available to you on line. You might not get every answer but at least you are asking the right questions.

This sort of general prep work is so easy to do and if we refer back to the model of goal-setting you could very easily give yourself an evening to look at the different routes, qualifications, requirements, big players, etc.

Using your extended network

I get that not everyone will be lucky enough to have loads of people upon whom they can rely to tap up for information so you may need to get a little creative. When you are trying to access people think about the following and who could possibly help. Start local to you; the people closest to you will be most inclined to help.

- **YOUR FAMILY -** does anyone in your family do this already? Do they know people who might? Do they work for a company that might have someone who does this?

- **YOUR FRIENDS** - do any of your friends have parents who are involved in this world? Might they work for a company that has this function?

- **YOUR TEACHERS** - do they have any links either through the school or personal connections to the area you want to study? In the example of accountancy, the school will have an accounts and finance department so there's at least one person you could speak to.

- **NEIGHBOURS** - if you're on friendly terms with any of them could they possibly steer you towards someone or be able to help?

- **ALUMNI NETWORK** - more and more schools are fostering links to their former pupils for just this purpose.

So, what now? Now you've got at least a couple of possible people you can speak to, you have the opportunity to ask questions, get work experience, pick their brains, ask about their route, ask about opportunities they may be aware of. This is all part of the process of filling in the blanks and getting a robust set of experiences that you can talk about as you progress your studies and career. Asking questions or favours from people who are already well disposed to you or have a vested interest in seeing you succeed should be the easiest thing in the world. But increasingly through the generations there is a temptation to remain hidden behind a desk trying to do everything remotely. When I was going through this stage in my life the internet was in its infancy. At my university if you wanted to use the internet you went to a huge room near the library with banks of PCs wired up to a shared modem. It was frankly much easier to get off your backside and go and ask someone than it was to wait for Jeeves to think about something for seven minutes before coming back with limited results. What that has meant is that there's an over-reliance on the internet. Students, our employees of the future, YOU are losing confidence in your people skills because they remain untested for most of your school career. So, in conclusion - the internet is great but has its limitations. Speaking to a person isn't keyword dependent; you can just chat and you may well learn a lot more about the reality of a situation or job. Don't neglect this.

As with the work experience we explored previously and with the informational interviewing we're about to look at, if you're asking people for help, try and be as clear as possible in advance about what you want to get from it. Depending on the relationship with the person, there will be a greater or lesser need for this but unless it's your parents there's no harm in going the formal route: take *it* seriously and they'll take *you* seriously.

Work experience

Obviously we covered this at some length in the previous chapter but, as you are, hopefully, beginning to discover, this is all part of the same big puzzle. Nnone of these things work in isolation; it all dovetails together in a very satisfying way.

Work experience, beyond all the benefits outlined before, gives you almost unparalleled access to knowledge and real-world versions of events. If we again take the accountant example, if I'm doing work experience at an accountants, I will literally be in an office with maybe twenty people, all of whom are doing what I want to do and are working at a variety of levels. This is like hitting the jackpot. Ask as many people as possible as much as you are able to soak up. Rinse and repeat, if you do only two or three work experience placements you are accessing the collective hive mind of accountancy or whatever else it is you want to do and you can learn huge amounts in a very limited period of time.

Informational interviewing

What now? Not really a skill or habit that we do either regularly or terribly well in the UK but it's all the rage in the USA and the Nordics. So what is informational interviewing? Simply put, it's a one-on-one conversation with someone who has a job you might like, who works within an industry you might want to enter, or who is employed by a specific company that you're interested in learning about and you are going to talk to them to get as much information as possible.

By this point you should have identified key people that you may wish to speak to, whether that's through your work experience, someone associated with the school, someone you've tracked down on-line - whoever and however you've found these people the following steps are crucial to the success or failure of this task:

- **Prepare for the interview**
  - Develop a short (15-30 second) overview of yourself, including your reasons for contacting this person, as a way to introduce yourself and define the context of the meeting.

  - Plan open-ended questions to ask - what do I mean by this? People aren't like Ouija boards: don't give them questions that require yes or no answers; ask them questions that require detailed responses. Only by doing this will you get them talking and make the most of your time.

- Initiate contact
  - Contact the person by phone or email.
  - Mention how you got his or her name.
  - Ask whether it's a good time to talk for a few minutes.
  - Emphasise that you are looking for *information, not a job.*
  - Ask for a convenient time to have a 20-30 minute appointment where you could come and see them.
  - Be ready to ask questions on the spot if the person says it is a good time for him/her and that s/he won't be readily available otherwise.

- Conduct the informational interview
  - Dress neatly and appropriately, as you would for a job interview.
  - Arrive on time or a few minutes early.
  - Restate that your objective is to get information and advice, not a job.
  - Give a brief overview of yourself and your education and/or work background.
  - Be prepared to direct the interview, but also let the conversation flow naturally, and encourage the interviewee to do most of the talking.

- Listen well and show genuine interest in what the person has to say.

- Take notes if you like, but do ask permission; no one wants to talk to the top of your head.

- Respect the person's time. Keep the appointment length within the time span that you requested.

- Ask the person if you may contact him or her again in the future with other questions.

- Always ask for names of other people to talk to for additional information or a different perspective.

TOP TIP: My old boss always used to say this to me when I was interviewing people - two ears, one mouth. You should do twice as much listening as talking. You know what you know, you want to know what they know.

- Follow-up

  - Keep records. Right after the interview write down what you learned, what more you'd like to know and your reactions in terms of how this industry, field or position would '"fit' with your lifestyle, interests, skills and future career plans.

  - Send a thankyou note within a couple of days to express your appreciation for the time and information given. Based on whether the informational interview was relatively informal or more businesslike, this may be a brief handwritten note, an email, or a business letter.

– Keep in touch with the person, especially if you had a particularly nice interaction. Let him or her know that you followed up on their advice and how things are going as a result. Take a view on how often this should be: too much can be needy and annoying but judge it right and this relationship could become an important part of your network.

Newspapers and trade magazines & related societies and associations

This is just good practice for the future in any case, but keeping abreast of the news is never a waste of time. Almost regardless of what your future may hold, the events that are happening around you may have an impact on what, how or where you do that thing. In the case of accountancy there may be legislative changes on income tax or corporation tax or a cut to working tax benefits or whatever it might be. Being up to speed on emerging stories or issues that have an effect on an industry or degree that you are interested in is helpful not just for conversations you might have, but also in the constant process of adjusting and refining your goals as you react to market changes. You might have always wanted to be a barrister but a few years ago they cut the budget for legal aid which had a knock-on effect on junior barristers and how much work was available to them which in turn would impact the short/medium term earning potential of anyone seeking out a pupillage. This, quite reasonably, could cause you to rethink your approach to entering the profession which in turn could impact the degree choice you'd make.

No matter what you want to do, be, study, learn about, the internet is filled with forums, associations and online publications. Linked In, for instance, is filled with groups that you can join and ask the members questions; so too is Facebook. All free at the point of access and offering a real opportunity to ask people working in your area of interest the questions you want answers to. Some others may require a membership fee, which, if you have the money to spare, is certainly worth considering, but there will be many more that are completely free and will give you access to current thinking on a wide range of issues and, in the forums, yet more opportunity to ask questions from people in the world already.

Conclusion

There may very well be other routes to information that I've not considered or included here and that you may uncover as you work your way through some of this stuff. Perhaps a business leader or a university or a company you're interested in is active on Twitter and they post regular, interesting tweets and articles. Whatever and however you get your information, the important thing is that you do. The better informed you are the better informed your choices become and the more knowledgeably you can discuss the area of interest. Plus you will have gained yet more skills talking to people in a professional environment, articulating your thoughts and building your professional network.

CASE STUDY
WAYNE HEMINGWAY

Wayne Hemingway is the owner and director of HemingwayDesign, a multi-disciplinary design house that incorporates urban and industrial design, clothing, furniture, building, graphic and brand design and curates art and community projects. He and his wife, Gerardine, started the fashion brand Red or Dead from a market stall in Camden. By the time they sold it they had featured at London Fashion Week many times over, had made vintage mainstream, had twenty-three shops worldwide, had won the first ever Street Style of the Year award from the British Fashion Council (an award they would go on to win another two times) and had made Dr. Martens a fashion item. They started the market stall to make their rent money for the week.

ME: You started in a band; that was your ambition. Was design something you had a particular interest in? Was it always an ambition? How did it come about?

WH: Obviously design was interesting for me, because of... just going out seeing bands all the time, dressing up and buying records and admiring their covers, that's all part of design. So, I was design aware. I was brought up in a designer way. It's just that the word design was never used; it was music and style.

ME: When you moved down to London, was it with the intention of making it big in music, or just for the experience of living in London?

WH: It was literally just that they had more nightclubs, I could see more bands. It was as simple as that. It was all based around being in a place to do the things that I wanted to do, which was to go out basically. To go clubbing.

ME: The story of taking all of your own clothes and going out to flog them to make rent, did you have a stall beforehand or was it literally just a case of you needed the money, let's see what happens?

WH: No, no, no stall at all beforehand. That was literally it. It wasn't everything we had, it was just a needs must situation. I didn't need everything in my wardrobe. Same as in life really, you don't need everything you've got. It was a need for money and that was the simplest way of getting money in my pocket to pay the rent, y'know, it's not rocket science.

ME: After the initial success you ended up with sixteen stalls - how did that come about? How did you get the capital to afford enough stock to supply sixteen stalls and how long did it take?

WH: Pretty quickly really. When you are at the beginning, when you're at the bottom of a curve, it can very suddenly start to take off. Because I'd always worn second-hand clothes, and there weren't many people doing it, I'd worked out how to do it. If you had £20 in your pocket back then you could've bought twenty dresses and you could sell each one for £20. Very, very easy to turn small amounts of cash into large amounts of cash. It was literally a licence to print money in those days. We couldn't believe what was happening, to tell you the truth. It was quite amazing.

ME: Were all the stalls around Camden or did you go across the rest of London as well?

WH: Well, Kensington, then Manchester, Affleck's Palace, The Royal Exchange in Manchester, then Liverpool: those were the places you could get cheap places to sell from. We just went at quite a pace doing that and opening all different places.

ME: Presumably you had to take on staff. Did it quite quickly go from being you and your wife into a 'proper' business?

WH: Oh yeah, we had to take on staff pretty quickly. Almost straight away.

ME: What drove that? Was it a particular ambition or was it reacting to the market? Would you describe yourself as being ambitious as such or was it more reactive?

WH: I think it's in most of us really. Once you get that chance to make money, it's kind of an instinct isn't it? If you've never had money then suddenly you start to make quite a lot of it and it's really good fun doing it. Doing something that's dead cool you just throw yourself into it. There was nothing else we could think of that was better to do.

ME: Was there never a temptation just to put your feet up when things were going well?

WH: We were young. At that age you have so much energy. We could see straight away that we had a chance to make a career that involved making the decisions that we wanted to make when we wanted to make them. Not feeling like you were going to work, even though it was work, is quite a good thing really. I'd see most of my family get up in the morning and not want to go to work, living for the weekend, and here we were counting the money and it didn't feel like you're going to work at all.

ME: As things progressed did you have a grand plan? Was there a final goal or point in your mind, or was it just seeing where this took you?

WH: No, never had anything like that. It was just... things just happened. Really, simply the case that things just happened and we went with the flow. It was just instinctive. We never thought, 'oh, let's do this' or 'let's plan this' or some grand plan to create a label that would show at London Fashion Week. It was do some clothes, then some shops, there's that thing called London Fashion Week, let's do a catwalk show. There were no advisors, nothing. Looking back it wasn't easy at all but at the time, because you've got the energy, it didn't seem that difficult. When you look back you do realise how hard you did work, and the people who worked with you remind you of the things that you did, like working through the night, but when you're in your early twenties and you're buying a house, and you compare yourself to your family - my nan and mum didn't buy their first houses until well into their forties. We're suddenly buying a house that was worth more than anyone we knew. It didn't seem like work then.

ME: What do you think gave you and your wife the edge?

WH: To sell what we sold, we were just about the first. There were people selling army surplus but there wasn't anyone really taking old pairs of jeans or old men's overcoats and certainly nobody selling old pairs of Dr. Martens: that was radical. To buy second-hand shoes, it was considered that only poor people did that. Our family definitely thought it was strange thing, almost a dirty thing to do. There was literally nobody else selling second-hand shoes on the scale we were doing it.

ME: Thinking about it, is there anything you would do differently in the current market? Would you try and set up on your own again?

WH: There's loads of things you could do differently but we might not have enjoyed it as much. I'm very happy with my lot, but if we'd wanted to become a world brand, I mean we had a lot of shops, we had twenty-three shops around the UK and around the world but if we'd wanted to become as big as someone like Ted Baker, or a cooler version of Ted Baker - he always said he based his business plan around *Red or Dead*, he was a big fan of *Red or Dead* - if we'd wanted to become that big, we could have borrowed money, we could have taken on other kinds of managers that had the experience to take you to that kind of level. I don't look back and think 'what if?' We had one of the biggest brands at the time. People would tell us how important it was and looking back I don't think we knew it: we were having fun, we were having kids, we never thought for a minute we should go to the market and borrow a few million quid and take on high powered accountants and marketing executives. It just didn't come to our minds really. I do know that if we had done that the brand would likely be massive by now.

ME: It does almost seem like that would be an anathema to the founding principles of the business.

WH: Yeah, it would have gone against the kind of people we are. We may've ended up unhappier, who knows? You can't go back and redo it.

ME: To anyone coming through now, thinking about the kind of challenges they are facing, is there anything you would say to them about entrepreneurship? Any advice?

WH: I think the main thing is, if you're going to start a business, if you don't enjoy it, it's probably not going to do that well. People watch these things on telly, like *The Apprentice* and they think, 'if I want to have a business and I have to come up with an idea', but it's not like that. Most businesses have come from people having a passion and doing what they want to do and would do it without the money, if you know what I mean. I think the most important thing is to want to do what you are doing.

ME: Thank you.

7

THE FRENCH DON'T EVEN HAVE A WORD FOR ENTREPRENEUR

'The best time to plant a tree was twenty years ago. The second best time is now.'

Chinese proverb

'If you just work on stuff you like and stuff you're passionate about, you don't have to have a master-plan with how things play out.'

Mark Zuckerberg

Now, many of you won't be aware as you were still quite young when it was all happening, but once upon a time before Donald Trump and even Barrack Obama was President, the USA voted in their millions to put someone who it's commonly agreed upon was a simpleton into the White House, George W. Bush, the son of the former President, George H.W. Bush. It's alleged that during a conversation with Tony Blair he announced that the problem with the French is that they didn't have a word for entrepreneur. This goes to show that even people without a functioning brain can hold the highest office in the world, so what's your excuse?

> **NOUN**
> noun: **entrepreneur**; plural noun: **entrepreneurs**
> a person who sets up a business or businesses, taking on financial risks in the hope of profit. 'many entrepreneurs see potential in this market'

So, what does the above mean to you and why is it so important? In simple terms it's just a handy label for people to throw around. I've set up and operated two businesses. I wouldn't describe myself as an entrepreneur as such; I just never really enjoyed working for anybody else. Many of you may already do things to make some money, maybe run a stall at a teenage market, sell things online etc etc. This is in essence what being an entrepreneur is, just on a smallish scale.

As we saw in the case study of Wayne Hemingway, he never had a big plan, he just enjoyed doing what he was doing and after a while he recognised that it could be a career - importantly for him a career where he and his wife were calling the shots rather than working for someone else. If you have a passion for something and that something can be used to make money, or if you're making money already, then congratulations - you're well on your way. The single largest obstacle to success is people not believing in themselves enough to take the risk and seeing it through. Bill Gates, Steve Jobs and Mark Zuckerberg, are all insanely wealthy and successful business people, all of whom dropped out of university to pursue their passion because they believed in it. Of course, Microsoft, Apple and Facebook all seem like sure bets now but at the time everyone was laughing at them, telling them they were wrong and stupid and irresponsible. What they did was back themselves to succeed and it's only by doing that that great and profound leaps in technology and science and everything else happen. Someone has to be willing to look foolish and say, 'I believe in this'.

I'm not saying you should drop everything and pursue a career in finger-painting because you're passionate about it but I am suggesting that success is a by-product of hard work, not an accident or coincidence. The luckiest people you meet are often the ones who work hardest. Being a self-starter, trying things, getting off your butt, is the surest way to find out who you are, what you like and, more importantly, who you want to be. You may not come up with the next big thing, but if you're trying you're more likely to get closer than the person who isn't.

By attempting and often failing at things you will learn a lot more about yourself, plus you will pick up a raft of skills, from problem solving to lateral thinking, market dynamics, marketing, supply chain issues, price points, selling and so on. These skills will serve you well no matter what you do and it all adds to the portfolio we are trying to build for you, so that when you enter the job market or apply for a place at university or an apprenticeship you will have a set of skills and experiences that are going to make you stand out from the competition.

Why is this important?

Business is changing, how we do business is changing, we as people are changing. My Dad would forever berate me and my brother for moaning about work: 'when did you get the idea that being happy is a right? Work's called work for a reason. Otherwise it'd be called fun.' Harsh, but entirely fair. Traditionally that is how the world has worked - but things are changing. Increasingly more and more emphasis is being placed on workplace happiness, staff satisfaction, and the work-life balance. More and more people are dropping out of the conventional workplaces to establish companies that are more attuned to what they want from their jobs. This is surely a very good thing but it throws up fresh challenges for you as you approach your futures.

In big companies there are a number of very clearly defined roles. It's a big machine and everyone has their part to play, they know what their part is and they get on and do it - so far so simple. As more and more smaller, less homogenised companies spring up, those roles become less defined so the Managing Director may well also be the sales and marketing person and be in charge of their website. The finance person may also do customer enquiries. Companies with ten or fewer employees are the new normal, and the ones with the highest happiness rates, and are increasingly becoming so. That means that, rather than training exclusively for one role that you will stick with throughout your career, you may need to develop a raft of skills and experiences that mean you can be used in a business across a number of areas.

An Australian think tank estimated that in the next twenty years or so we would see a number of traditional positions; as much as 60 per cent, being lost to automation. Oxford University has just published a similar report. A business leader wrote an article listing the first five jobs to disappear when the robots take over. We see it already in manufacturing; even in supermarkets it's happening where we scan our own shopping.

On top of which, as old industries die and new ones emerge, a lot of traditional professions will die with them. Don't let that scare you. Obviously there will always be a need for certain core skills and professions even if the manner in which they are utilised will change and evolve. The important thing is to be aware that the changes are coming and by developing soft skills, by being a self-starter and having a greater range of experiences you will much better insulate yourself against the changes and it will give you a greater range of opportunities. Being able to adapt and react to changes in the employment market is the essence of Darwinism; it will give you greater longevity and increased options.

So that's why it's important for the wider job market, but also it's important because you *might* invent the next big thing. If not now, when? As we said previously, you've the rest of your life to compromise. Now, when you have nothing but opportunity, you should be trying things, exploring your options, putting yourself out there. Daring to fail. Whatever that thing is that you're passionate about, why aren't you trying to make that your career today? Say it's football: you could set up a coaching and skills afternoon for kids. Say it's computers: design an app. If it's photography, take pictures, take them to galleries, promote them online. Never before in history has it been so easy to market yourself for free to such a huge potential audience. All the social media stuff we looked at before is a global market stall that you could be accessing right now.

'Entrepreneur' in the context of this chapter is less about setting up a business but rather a mindset that you can develop and work on throughout your career.

So, in the context of you and why this is important, no one expects you to start your own business, to risk everything in pursuit of your dream, but don't falsely cling to the idea that there is a 'safe' route any more. Things are changing and by being adaptable, learning and trying things, taking risks, as weird as it seems, may be much safer in the long term. Fortune favours the bold.

8

HOW NOT TO HIDE YOUR LIGHT UNDER A BUSHEL

'Modesty: the gentle art of enhancing your charm by pretending not to be aware of it.'
Oliver Herford

'False modesty can be worse than arrogance.'
David Mitchell

No matter what or where you choose to go when you leave the hallowed halls of your school, some truths are universal. You will, at some point, have to write a CV or an application form. Benjamin Franklin may as well have put it down on his list of inevitabilities alongside death and taxes. Working in recruitment for as long as I have and do, I have seen something in the region of 100,000 CVs. Sounds ridiculous right? Twenty-five to thirty CVs a day, 260 working days a year, for fourteen-plus years. It adds up. Working as an academic consultant I have seen many, many personal statements. So, when a teacher tries to instruct a student on how to write a CV or personal statement and considers their job done and that box ticked, it makes me laugh. Not like a genuine laugh at a friend's joke but rather a bitter, hollow laugh. You guys are getting a raw deal and most, if not all, schools are failing to use genuine experts in the field. Even a manager from a local business will likely only see a handful of CVs in any given year, as they will have been vetted, checked and filtered before they reach their inbox, and your guidance counsellor is unlikely to have been on the other side of the table when it comes to working out whether an application is good or bad. So next time a teacher tells you what to write on your CV or how to construct a personal statement designed to sell YOU, consider the source.

Before we tackle the 'how tos' let's consider the 'whats'. In its most basic form the CV or personal statement or application form is just a breakdown of your experiences chronologically. This is what you will have been taught and shown, and yes, sure, they encourage you to dress it up a little but it's normally riddled with clichéd drivel. If I read on just one more CV that someone is adept as both a team player as well as being able to work on their own, it's possible I may gouge my own eyes out. Think about what that actually says and consider whether it's worth bragging about. 'I can behave myself around other people without being unnecessarily difficult and don't require constant babysitting if on my own.' If these are the most positive attributes you can muster to justify why you should be granted a place or a job then your only chance is if the pickings are pretty slim for those making the choices. However, they are not. The job market and places at the best universities and apprenticeships are increasingly competitive and the capacity to not misbehave unless permanently supervised is not the selling point it once was.

Any time you are asked to commit your experiences and abilities to paper is an opportunity to sell yourself. It is, in essence, a marketing brochure designed to woo and tease the reader into wanting to know more about you, at least enough to open the door for you to get in front of them and seal the deal in person.

We're going to go through the best way to create a personal statement and a CV- that's not to deny the importance of an application form but, with so many differences, it'd be impossible to create a comprehensive 'how to.' Most, if not all, of the issues thrown up by an application form will be addressed in the other two formats.

The Killer personal statement

Where to begin? When confronted with a blank page and no idea where to start, it can be pretty daunting. A good rule of thumb is to begin with extensive note-taking, thinking back through your experiences and jotting down any and all things that you believe may be relevant. Remember, by the point you are writing this you will have a distinct end point in mind; at least you will have selected a course. This gives you a real advantage because it allows you to disregard everything else that doesn't serve to create a narrative that supports your desire to reach that goal.

The issue every student faces at this point is that for the most part you will all have had pretty similar experiences. You will have gone to school, maybe have been on some teams, done a play, done DoE or NCS, and now you are applying for a place at a university. There is nothing remarkable or noteworthy in your background because logically the people who are applying to the same course as you will likely have similar interests to you and therefore will have pursued similar activities to you, so it's a level playing ground that will be decided by grades. Which is great if you're going to get straight A*s, but for the rest of you it's pretty much the luck of the draw.

Set against that backdrop, it begins to highlight how important a good personal statement can be - in the States certainly, and increasingly here, there is ever greater weight being given to the personal statement, partially because the teachers do such an adequate job of comprehensive homogenisation of the student body to the point they are all the same (on paper), and partially because they are now approaching admissions on a more holistic, class-wide basis. The universities are trying to ensure that the character and mix of any incoming class is going to be one that pushes and challenges another and, longer term, creates a stronger and more successful bunch of graduates that will go on to great things, creating a better legacy for the university.

So, how can you avoid being just one of many in a faceless sea of same? Well if you've read the book through from the start to here you already know the answers. If you skipped a few chapters then go back and start at the beginning! What makes you the most interesting and compelling version of you is the experiences you've gained, the insights you've earned, the recommendations you've acquired through the extra curricular activities, work experiences, informational interviewing and so on that you've done. Simply put, the experiences you've worked at getting over the last year, two years etc are the things that make you different; your unique qualities and insights are something that no one else will have, because they are yours. The trick is to turn those experiences into statement gold.

Schools will tell you that universities are looking for all-rounders: people who have been on sports teams, been in school plays, been in a couple of clubs and societies and so on. But that's a fallacy. No university wants someone who's average at lots of things: they want someone who is exceptional at one thing. If you're studying English Literature, do you really imagine they care that you were in 3rd team hockey? Of course they don't! It would be like applying for a job as a mechanic and explaining that you could make an omelette. It in no way factors into their thinking. If you are applying to study a subject at the highest level then the people responsible for making that decision are looking for evidence of your ability to do it, your commitment to the subject and your capacity to see it through to the end. If they feel for a moment that you are lukewarm, half-hearted, or lack sincerity regarding your commitment to the subject, why would they bother offering you a place? Selling yourself is about understanding your audience - you sell to what that audience wants.

Obviously, each university, course and tutor will have a different view about what they want and how they want to be sold to, so again think about your research. Other people who have successfully got on that course will probably have blogged about it somewhere. Check it out, not to steal their ideas/essays but just to be better informed about what worked for them; any insights are always useful.

NOW WHAT? Here's a checklist you should be able to satisfy before you even lift a biro to scribble some notes with:

1) Know what you want to study.

Self-evident really, but you cannot possibly sell yourself effectively if you don't know who your audience is and you are deeply committed to and passionate about what you are saying. Read about the courses, modules etc, as it'll make it easier to figure out whether it's the right course for you, but, from a statement perspective, you can better explore how your experiences map onto and fit against what they offer. All of this helps you sell yourself better.

2) Pays your money, takes your choices (up to 5).

Make them count. With only five choices to go at, make sure you choose courses and universities that your predicted grades would give you a shot at getting into. Be realistic: if you wildly over-achieve, you could always take a year out to do something interesting and reapply for the following year. Putting all your eggs in one basket, whilst brave, could be foolish; the universities themselves don't see who else you've applied to so it won't demonstrate unwavering commitment to them and could leave you in the shallow end of the pool with no swimsuit.

3) What if your choices are different?

Most people tend to spread their bets across the universities with similar courses; obviously it makes it much easier to write a compelling statement if you are selling to the same kind of audience. Where it can all get a little unnecessary is when you choose wildly conflicting courses and the statement can then seem quite off-kilter. In this instance it would be advisable to seek outside counsel - I've included a few thoughts at the end of the chapter but it's a sticky wicket. Don't throw a random one in there just to mix it up unless you are serious about it. The risk is the audience reading it: unless you've been super slick in marrying wildly different thoughts into a universally appealing narrative, they may just disregard you as you being a lunatic without the first idea of what you want to do.

4) The exception that proves the rule.

Obviously many of you will be thinking about applying for joint or combined honours: Law with French, or Business Studies and Psychology, or anything else you can think of. These are the courses whereby you can marry two different ideas and make them part of the same narrative. 'Having an innate understanding of how people operate, what makes them tick will, I believe, give me an advantage within the business setting.' Obviously bland and banal, but it serves to illustrate how you can link two subjects, knit them together to create a cohesive narrative.

5) Cats, teeth and bodies

Sitting outside the usual rules are those rare and highly specialised courses: veterinary medicine, dentistry and medicine. You are allowed a maximum of four choices but, given how competitive these are, it may be worth throwing a fifth different one into the mix. Bear in mind that the Big Three are pretty pleased with themselves and won't take kindly to a diluted version of your statement, so it's worth choosing a course that would still make sense of the statement to a tutor. For instance, if you chose four medicine courses and the fifth was biomedical sciences, references to wanting to be a doctor in the future wouldn't seem out of place. A fifth unrelated course that bears no relevance to your statement however could just be a squandered choice.

What next? You've done your research, you've seen what others have had to say about their own experiences and you've wracked your brain to come up with all the useful and relevant examples and thoughts that seek to demonstrate your interest and commitment to the subject. Now, you need to start to order it into a compelling, articulate and passionate narrative that effectively sells who you are and what this means to you and why.

In thinking about what to include and what to reject it may be prudent to consider what admissions tutors themselves hate to see. Every year I see the same clichéd, rote banalities and every year the universities explain how much they hate seeing them. Do yourself a favour and don't wilfully annoy them from the word go. Below are some key gripes that come up time and again and can easily be avoided.

- **QUOTATIONS -** with only 4000 characters to play with, don't squander your space using quotes that the tutors could read anywhere else and probably have done several times, most likely in other personal statements. They want to know about you and what you have to say. It's a lazy crutch: one which I've used throughout the book, but then I don't have to limit my word count.

- **IRRELEVANT, CONTEXTLESS THOUGHTS -** simply listing all the countries you've been to, work experience placements, films that changed your life, etc, is not a fun thing to read. It's like reading a grocery list. As we explored in previous chapters, work experience without actually learning something from it is simply being somewhere a bit different for a few hours. When you detail the experiences you've had you need to make them count for something, otherwise the whole thing's been a waste. Give it context: why is it relevant to the course? What did you learn from it, either about yourself, your goals, the subject? And so on. Make it mean more than just something you once did.

- **WEIRD, UNNATURAL LANGUAGE -** one of the big issues admissions tutors flag up is when it all seems too polished. The personal statement is of course an opportunity to sell yourself but it's also an opportunity for the reader to get an idea of who you are and what your hopes and ambitions are. The more unnatural and polished it is, the less authentic it becomes. Write from the heart and try to avoid antiquated words that you wouldn't use in real life. Firstly, there's the risk you might get it slightly wrong and misuse a word and, secondly, if you have to interview and 'paper you' doesn't stack up to 'fleshy you' when you speak in real life, it's going to put a question mark over your head.

- **CLICHÉS -** almost too many to mention but speak to your peers and you can pretty much guarantee at least a few of the following: 'The world today is',

'Ever since I was young', 'I've always been fascinated by' and so on. 'Passion/passionate' and 'fuelled my desire to X' are another two perennial offenders. They are meaningless, trite, a waste of characters, and are the linguistic equivalent of a place-holder. It tells them nothing and doesn't help you.

- **UNSUBSTANTIATED LIES AND BRAGGING -** firstly, bragging - selling yourself - is not the same thing as making wild, unsubstantiated claims. Making grand proclamations about what you excel at, why you believe you are the best thing since bread came sliced, why your achievements are so impressive - these all invite the world-weary tutor to call you out. Show, don't tell. If your achievements are that impressive they will speak for themselves. People want evidence and facts, not unsupported self-congratulatory whooping. Secondly, lies and, more importantly, plagiarism - UCAS has very good software aimed at stopping people copying, cribbing or otherwise nicking vast chunks of statement - it might seem easy but you WILL get caught. Lies, half truths and deceptions are easily disproved, particularly around certain experiences: speaking a language, a book you might claim to love, etc. If you don't speak the language or didn't finish the book, don't say you did.- If you get quizzed on it at interview, there's no way back from that.

- **GAGS -** the trouble with jokes, humour, quirkiness, is that they are very subjective: you don't know who exactly will read your statement and the chances are pretty strong that they will not share the same sense of humour as you. In an interview, where you can respond to them, gauge their reactions, and respond to their body language, by all means employ humour as a tactic, but in a statement it's too risky. Even if they don't actively dislike the joke, is it worth the risk and the space used? Better to be slightly more conformist than throw it all away with a misjudged line.

- **IRRELEVANCIES -** I said it at the top and I say it again, every letter counts. Unless something actively enhances the essay and serves the narrative you are trying to create, then bin it. As you read through, try and apply the shrug test: if there's any part of you that thinks that someone who doesn't know you would read through this and shrug, scrap it.

- **YOU HAVE TO ACCENTUATE THE POSITIVES -** people sometimes mistake negativity for humility; don't focus on the things that didn't go your way or ruefully describe missed opportunities. Remember this is a sales document: sell yourself and frame your experiences in the most positive way possible. You want to do science - you conducted an experiment that trashed your hypothesis? That's great! Think about all the things you learned from that, not 'and that was that'.

Those are the big pitfalls you have to avoid and it's important to know them before you launch into your statement. So now you know what not to do, what do you need to include? What's going to get you noticed for the right reasons and what should you try and focus on?

Some of the greatest speeches, novels and films have an absolute juggernaut of an opener and many students have hanged themselves on trying to capture that lightning and bottle it. Getting the opening right may seem like the most crucial part of the whole statement and yes, of course it's important, but rather than become pole-axed trying to get that killer sentence, think of the essay as a whole, fill in the blanks, and the rest, including the opening, should start to piece together. Most admissions tutors agree that honesty and directness is as compelling as a flashy opening; they aren't looking for gimmicks but rather for you to engage them with your thoughts and ideas on the subject and why it matters to you. Things to think about for your opening paragraph:

- Don't try too hard to be different and eye-catching: you can go overboard without realising it and put people off.

- Explain what set you off on the path, what about the course/subject excites you and why you are interested in it.

- Get to the point quickly. Don't waste space and time with fluff. Be specific and targeted.

- Be natural, they want to get to know you and the words you choose are how you represent yourself to them.

- The first two sentences should cover what you want to study and why, what excites you, why you want to learn more and what you hope to accomplish with that knowledge. Crucially, you need to explain what you find interesting/ exciting about it. It's not enough just to say it is interesting; why? What do you want to prove, solve, contribute to?

- Keep it relevant. Like with the *X Factor* that we discussed before, when a fifteen year old says, 'I've been singing since I was a little kid' it lacks any impact. Don't talk about history, talk about you now. What's inspiring your choices today? Was it a single issue, experience or problem that you feel passionately about? Get it down!

As you start to piece together anecdotes and examples that serve the same structure we keep coming back to, you'll see the beginning seems less and less important. My temptation would be to approach it as if you are writing a number of short paragraphs covering different experiences and then weave them together so they all blend into one complete document that speaks to who you are, what you hope to accomplish, why the course is interesting, and demonstrates that you have a long-standing interest and commitment to that subject and aspirations to pursue a future in it.

> The main thrust of the first draft is just to capture as much of that raw enthusiasm as possible: unvarnished, unedited you. You can primp and preen it later.

All of which is a long-winded way of saying, the killer opener is a bit of a white elephant. If you've got a strong one, then great, but don't kill yourself trying to manufacture one; honesty and openness are just as effective. As before, lay off the quotes: a lot of people think they add profundity to the beginning of an essay; they don't. They serve to highlight your lack of confidence in your own thoughts and opinions.

Some people recommend 'closing the loop' - this is exactly as it sounds, bringing the essay full circle. If you are starting with a strong message about what has motivated you to do X, then reiterating the same point at the end can be an effective rejoinder that underpins the same message.

That's the opening covered - what about everything else?

The cunning thing about the personal statement is that it very cleverly includes a big clue as to what you should be aiming for when you write it – make it 'personal'. That's the key to its success or failure. Ignoring that key word in favour of hyperbole and quotes and clichés can mean the difference between whether you get that spot on your dream course or whether the person you are competing with does. It comes down to that stark a choice. No more are grades on their own king. Realistically, if you take as read that which I said before - that most students will have very similar stories and experiences - it stands to reason that grades-wise too, there won't be much to choose between you. Given that people make their course selection on predicted grades, it's not a stretch to assume that most people applying to the same course as you will have similar predicted grades and that is where the statement is your last best hope.

1) Why this?

Explain your reason for wanting to study this course, what has motivated you to make the decision to pursue this further, demonstrate your long-standing enthusiasm and dedication to it. If you've a particular goal or outcome you're working towards it may be helpful to say so. Be specific and to the point; no one likes waffle, plus you don't have the room.

2) Why you?

It's not enough or a given that because you're enthusiastic you should be offered a place: that should be the very minimum expectation. What about you, beyond being keen, is going to make you a good bet for the tutor to take a chance on? How are you right for the course? Show that you understand the nature of the course/subject/profession, that you can hit the targets and level they expect and that you grasp the rigour required to succeed at university and that you know why you want to do it in the first place. Demonstrating you know what is required without making brash statements about the fact that you know is tricky to get right, but as before the more you can show rather than tell the better. *Eg, 'I understand that a big part of being a contracts manager is building relationships with clients; the experience I gained whilst working in X has helped me develop some of those soft skills that I believe may be useful in my future career.'*

3) This is me and why should you care?

Now you can break out all those wonderful and exciting stories about the experiences you've had and reflect on how what you learned has impacted your thinking, your views, your opinions; what you've gained from them and how you believe they will positively impact how you will conduct yourself on the course and how you will apply that learning. You can namecheck books, articles, films, thinkers that changed the way you looked at things but be specific. Writing a list isn't helpful, it requires context: why is that relevant and how does it help the tutor gain a better idea of who you are? Try to avoid being populist: everyone cites Freakonomics; don't be that person. This is the heavy ammo of the statement, a real chance to show your interest, understanding and commitment to a subject.

4) Going pro

Some, but not all, courses are intrinsically linked to a career. If you study veterinary medicine there's a fair chance you want to be a vet. Demonstrate an understanding of where this could take you and what you want to go on to do, along with any insights you've gained about the profession. Particularly the skills/qualities you've identified as necessary to be successful and how/what you've done to try and acquire and develop them, as well as why you feel it's important and vital and interesting etc., shows (not tells) someone who is in it for the long haul.

5) What else?

They don't expect you to know everything on day one but what else can you bring to the table? We talked before about the skills and abilities you don't recognise as being linked to any specific subject. Now's the chance for them to shine. How can these soft skills be transferred into this course? Problem solving, leadership, public speaking, listening, organising - whatever those previously intangible qualities are, if they can be made relevant then demonstrate how and when you've used them and why that might be desirable to the course leader. Again, don't just list 'qualities' you might have - be focused and use them wisely; it's all helpful when done well. Be specific and targeted, give examples: it's no good just saying you're an inspirational leader, show them a time when you've inspired and led. Give them examples and draw conclusions; it shows your capacity to understand what you've learned and apply it practically.

6) Got the chops?

By showing them that you are capable of independently getting work experience and then drawing conclusions, you tacitly sell them on the idea that you have the capacity for critical thinking, working off your own back, analysing those experiences to yield conclusions and original thoughts. Something like the EPQ (Extended Project Qualification) is a good example but all your experiences and skills that you've developed if you've drawn conclusions and learnt things from it, show the capacity for analytical thinking and independent study.

7) Got to keep the energy up

Remember positive framing: keep the tone upbeat, optimistic about the future. Posturing about how things are terrible but you've got the solutions is a brassy move but probably not a sensible one.

8) Where does it all end?

In the same way that passion for the course is important, so too is passion for the career that it can lead you towards. If you've an exciting goal in your head it might seem far-fetched, but if you can explain what you want to do and how you intend to get there that becomes instantly compelling. Be inspired though: a dull walk-through of the steps you might take in order to become an accountant isn't exciting. If you don't have a job in mind, stick to the medium term. What are you hoping university will give you and what experiences do you feel you might gain? If you're thinking of taking a gap year, make sure you've got a firm plan and explain to them how what you're going to do will further deepen your understanding of the course you intend to take or how it will help you grow as person. Make them understand it is structured and worthy of your efforts and their patience.

A very brief guide to anyone hoping to create a personal statement aimed at wildly differing audiences because of the choices made (or making one statement work for multiple courses)

I would never recommend this as I think it shows a lack of clarity of thought and through-vision and the worry is that the universities will see it similarly and you'll fall between two stools., But equally I understand that you may find yourself being torn between two distinct and equally desirable options. The best advice I can offer is to approach the university or specific admissions tutors directly and explain your issue: they may allow for you to write a statement specifically for that course. If in doubt, ask. Better to be told no than plough on regardless.

It remains possible to write compellingly about similar subjects that share a certain theme and end point, but if you try and be too catch-all and generic, if the gaps are too broad to broach, the likelihood is that you'll put off everyone equally.

That's a lot to take in and there's still probably a thousand conflicting opinions and bits of advice out there, but as a general rule of thumb all of the above is broadly the combined wisdom of lots of different advisors, tutors, coaches and admissions people's current thinking on best practice. There are a number of courses and universities that look for quite specific things, either in addition to or to the exclusion of some that I've detailed. This should be covered in Phase 1's research though.

The key things to remember –

Be honest.

Be yourself.

Don't quote.

Make the words count.

Show, don't tell, what you can offer.

Sell the idea of you as an interesting, interested asset.

Explain how the experiences you've had have given you skills and knowledge that has been earned and can be applied to the course.

Your hopes and ambitions for the course and your future.

How to write the KILLER CV

Well this is right in my wheelhouse. You may have thought my treatise on the personal statement was hugely impressive - and you'd be right - but the CV, oh, you are in for a treat! Where to start? Well I guess the best place is understanding the point of a CV. Like a personal statement, it is a sales document, a marketing brochure, an advert, in essence. Unlike a personal statement, you don't have the luxury of flowery prose, talking about what inspires you and your hopes for the future. It is much more factual, drier and concise.

Like universities, every company or role you may be applying for has its own character and clear views on what might work for them culturally, their own view on the sort of personality that will fit in, certain types of experience that are favoured above others, and you must sell to that need. Any and all recruitment is predicated on the idea that there is an issue, problem or gap that needs be solved, resolved or filled; they are hoping you can be that person as it takes a problem off their plate. Your job in both the CV and interview is to offer them the confidence that you can be that solution.

Naturally, as you stand here, at the beginnings of your career there will be a much greater reliance on your potential and personality rather than your years of experience, but tailoring your CV to a specific audience and selling to a specific need is a good habit to get into and one which you should practise every time you apply for a role. Remember, in a competitive market very slim margins can mean the difference between success and failure, so take the time to do it right and treat each application as thoroughly as you can.

Where to start?

Regardless of where you want to apply, you should create for yourself a basic template that can be tweaked according to your audience. This template should as standard include the following -

- Name and address, contact details.

- Executive summary.

- Education.

- Work experience.

- Additional qualifications.

- Interests.

- References.

The importance and weighting of these will naturally change and evolve as you progress through your career, so things like interests will matter less. For example, if you're in your forties and applying for a post as an electrical engineer, the fact you enjoy Mongolian throat-singing is probably less important than your degree in electrical engineering and twenty years' experience of working as an electrical engineer.

Name and address, contact details

Self-explanatory: list your name and address at the top of the page, along with pertinent contact details. This highlights the need for a sensible email address (as I mentioned earlier); if it's on top of your CV it needs to be professional. A lot of people put their age which is not only entirely unnecessary but it is actively frowned upon. After a change in the law regarding age discrimination, recruitment consultants cannot even allude to a candidate's age when representing someone into a business. Furthermore, they have to remove the dates when the candidate studied so an employer can't estimate from when they were at school. It's not a critical thing to remember at this age - the nature of the roles you'll be applying for and absence of experience will age you anyway - but it's worth bearing in mind for the future.

Executive summary

This is the one opportunity you have to exercise anything like artistic licence. Increasingly popular in CVs nowadays, the executive summary/personal statement, however you choose to label it, is a brief overview of who you are, what you can offer and what you have done. At the start of your career this is going to be more about the potential you have, your ambitions and your commitment to a certain area. As you gain additional experiences, it will become more about what you have done and what you can offer. This is also the single largest portion of the CV that can be altered to sell to a specific need. For instance, if you were applying for a role that was sales focused you would tweak it to amplify your experience working with customers, building relationships and selling; if it were more about working with people, you would emphasise your exposure to team working, collaborative things you've done. Certain words and phrases can help you subtly adjust the template to work for your desired audience.

In the summary that you will write today, much greater weighting will be given to this portion over the work experience portion because necessarily most of your time has been spent at school, leaving less time for work - what you are hoping to sell the audience on is that the experiences you've had in school are transferable into a professional environment. Where you need to be careful is in hyperbole. I work with and have seen a lot of students' CVs and they make pretty bold claims and use wildly superlative adjectives to describe pretty meagre achievements. If you describe yourself as 'funny' or 'great with people' or 'a natural leader' you are asking people to prove you wrong. It seems conceited, even more so when you are younger, and these are not only subjective but largely untested claims. As with the personal statement, think about how you can demonstrate these qualities, rather than tell them you have them.

One of my biggest bugbears with a CV, and one that I know frustrates a lot of employers, is when people write about themselves in the third person. You want to avoid saying I too much, but it's a hell of a lot better than 'Sharon is an inspiring dog impersonator' or whatever it might be; it just makes it look like Sharon is either incapable of writing her own CV or that she might enter a room and announce that Sharon is pleased to meet you. It sounds weird, so avoid it at all costs. If in doubt, just avoid pronouns.

Think about what your essential qualities are and try and distil them into a pithy paragraph or two. Remember who your audience is and choose appropriate adjectives for that market. Also remember that a lot of what you are selling is your enthusiasm and potential. Don't try to be something you're not - it makes you look a little ridiculous. Let's look at an example to help contextualise it -

PROFILE

I'm ambitious and entrepreneurial and, although currently studying for my A levels, I also run my own jam-making business and have done so for the last three years. Following a gap year I intend to study leisure and tourism at university and specialise in catering. To gain additional experience, I am attending a cookery course arranged via the local college. I believe the skills I have gained through running my own business have given me a real-world insight into the demands of the workplace and feel confident that this, combined with my focus and ambition, would mark me out as someone with true potential who can really deliver.

This is a solid example of how to position your key qualities: it introduces the fact you have some experience of a real business and demonstrates ambition, entrepreneurship and suggests that you have picked up additional skills. Critically, you are upselling the idea that the skills and benefits of having worked for yourself will make you a better employee because you understand some of the challenges and will have encountered some of the issues and learned how to deal with them.

What you don't want to do is spend too long talking about how your business is your passion etc. When someone is looking for an employee they aren't looking for someone who has got one foot out of the door; they want to know you are focused on them and what their goals are. What this statement does is present an insight into what their longer term plans are, but not in a way that countermands the short term offering and sells to a catering/tourism type role.

If we are creating a broader template for use when applying for a role where you don't have a specific interest or experience, an alternative version might be something like this -

Wendy is seventeen and currently attends Generic High School's sixth form where she is studying A levels in English Language, Art, Media and General Studies. She is an enthusiastic and reliable young adult with a very outgoing personality, and is comfortable communicating with young people of all ages, as well as adults. Wendy is an extremely keen runner who has represented her school, city and county in numerous events, and intends to develop a career in the TV and media industry.

Only - eurgh, right? What is wrong with this? Almost too many things to mention. Yes, it is earnest and sincere, but also completely off-putting.

- Use of the third person. When you see it in an example, hopefully you'll get how jarring it is.

- The age - irrelevant.

- 'Very outgoing' - firstly how does one measure the difference between outgoing and very outgoing? Secondly it invites challenge.

- Comfortable communicating with young people of all ages... oh, how big of Wendy! She condescends to speak to people she goes to school with.

- Keen runner. Good but lacks context and relevance.

- Intends to develop a career in the TV and media industry - unless this job is linked to or relevant for that industry, it's unclear why she would alert them to the fact she will always be looking elsewhere. Also, given that she doesn't state where in that industry she wants to be, it smacks of saying, 'I just wanna be famous'.

Let's try that statement again and see if the same essential facts can be parlayed into something that is less off-putting and can create a broader appeal.

> An enthusiastic, outgoing and ambitious student, currently working towards my A levels in English Language, Art, Media and General Studies. As a county level athlete I believe I understand what it takes to succeed in any given environment, it takes commitment, determination and hard work - all areas I have proven myself in. Working as part of an elite team alongside my academic commitments I have developed a number of transferable skills including communication, time-management and listening, skills I hope to further develop in the professional sphere.

Same essential facts but re-framed in a way that is less self-congratulatory and more relevant to a general audience. What you should be striving for in your summary template is something that sells you but doesn't put people off. Focus on the transferable skills: if you don't currently work then think of the skills and experiences you've acquired elsewhere and how they could be useful in a work setting. You'll note that I've left off the stuff about media entirely; now we're using media as an example but, like with a personal statement, try and stay on message; unless the role is connected in some way to your aspirations it's not really worth inclusion.

Experience

Straightforward enough, in chronological order from the most recent, give the reader an overview of what you've been up to. This is where the work experience, shadowing, etc. is particularly useful - otherwise you don't really have anything to say. But assuming you did and do then this is a solid way to display it:

Owner, Jammy Sod; Anywhereshire
2013 - Present

I set up and developed my own company, Jammy Sod, a bespoke jam-making business. I have run this business for three years now, and sell regularly at farmers' markets, artisan markets and craft fairs. I have a number of people who work with me so we can have a presence at numerous markets concurrently. I am responsible for making the jam, taking and making orders, and online marketing through social media, in addition to which I am currently building a website.

Assistant, Typical Business; Anywhereshire
2013 - Present

Working for the family's model cheese practice I perform a range of administrative duties such as organising files, answering phones and generally ensuring all of my co-workers have what they need to do their job smoothly.

Volunteer, Local Soup Kitchen; Town Centre
2014

During the time I spent at the Soup Kitchen, I spent a number of days completing a variety of tasks. I was responsible for cleaning, some general prep work and serving. I worked as part of a team to ensure we did this efficiently and sensitively.

Now, for someone at this age, this is more than most employers would expect. As you progress through your career you incorporate more of your achievements and success that you enjoyed in each role. A good rule of thumb for the future is breaking down what your key responsibilities are and then how you succeeded in that role by meeting those responsibilities and excelling. But for now, just cover the bases.

A lot of people at your age who have started their own businesses give themselves wildly inflated titles like Managing Director, or Marketing Director or Lord Business. Keep it simple: it doesn't look impressive, it looks a bit like a toddler wearing grown-up shoes. I don't say that in a patronising way at all - any teenager who has the gumption to get up and start a business has my unwavering respect - but the fact you've done it is evidence enough of your initiative and ambition. You don't need to hide behind big titles: be proud of what you've accomplished.

Importantly, a lot of people in CVs use bullet points etc, and often will brag about having an eye for detail, being conscientious and so on. Whatever you do, ensure it's consistent - dates in the same place, same format, full stops on everything, spellchecked and so on.

Also, less important now, but useful to remember for the future, employers will look negatively on someone who moves from job to job very quickly - it doesn't offer them confidence that they will stick around. When doing dates, use month and year. 2013-2016 looks good, but if it's Dec 2013

- Jan 2016, it tells quite a different story; if you don't include months it can look like you're tying to hide something.

Education

No great secrets here: get it down and make it neat – again, as you progress through your career, less and less weighting will be given to your GCSEs and more and more to your experiences and the highest academic awards you got.

Generic High School, Anywhereshire — A level / AS level, September 2015 - June 2017

I am currently working towards my A levels in English Literature, Art, English Language and my AS in General Studies. My predicted grades are: AAAA (why not?).

Generic High School, Anywhereshire — GCSE, June 2013 - June 2015

I gained GCSEs in Personal Finance (A*), Fine Art (A), History (A), Physical Education (B), Geography (B), Biology (B), Chemistry (B), French (B), English Language (C) and English Literature (C).

Again, note the formatting: neat and regular. A lot of people seem to write their grades in a big ol' list right down the centre of the page; this takes up far too much room and, unless the grades are exceptional, you are wanting people to buy into your skills and experiences so don't make it a half page feature.

Additional Qualifications

This is essentially a chance to show off other skills and abilities you might have. This could be your Duke of Edinburgh award, life-saving certificate, driving licence, EPQ, NCS, additional languages, etc. Whatever extra curricular stuff you have in the mix that you think may be of interest to a potential employer, this is your chance to stick it in.

> I am confident with a range of IT packages - Word, PowerPoint, Publisher, email. I am an active member of the school leadership team, which requires me to arrange school activities, including prom and charity events. I also recently completed my Gold DofE award and have a full clean driving licence.

Alternatively you can make it a more businesslike -

- IT confident, including - Word, PowerPoint, Publisher, email.

- Gold Duke of Edinburgh award.

- Member of School Leadership Team.

- Full clean driving licence.

Neither is more right than the other. The first is more personal and offers a little more in the way of the personality alongside the facts, the second is more straightforward - both can work well as long as they remain consistent with the rest of the CV. The best way to judge would be on the nature of the job you're applying for: is the company young and exciting and all wow and shiny? Or is it a more staid, formal business setting? Both examples can work for either, but try and get a sense of what they are looking for in their advert (often the job advert can give you a big clue in how they phrase what they are looking for in a person.)

Interests

As we touched on earlier, these are much less important as an adult where your experience will do most of the talking for you but, with minimal experience to go on, an employer will be keen to get to know you and this is the last opportunity to make a less formal version of the summary covering less of the work-you and more of the you-you.

> I am a keen runner and have represented my county in cross-country, I also play field hockey for a local club where I am club secretary - I very much enjoy being part of a team and working together for a common goal.

That would pretty much do it. A lot of people - and by 'a lot' I mean almost every CV I've seen - have put a list of utterly banal interests. Whatever you do, don't put 'I enjoy socialising with my friends' - everyone does, otherwise they wouldn't be your friends! It's like writing you have skin; same goes for 'I enjoy going to the cinema', 'keen gym goer' and so on. This always comes across like you're trying to convince someone you're a real person, you do something fun, but hey, you also take your health seriously... if you're going to say you love reading, be warned, you'd better had. The people who don't love reading will never ask you about it; the people who do will, which means one thing: they are probably literary snobs otherwise they wouldn't ask. So if they ask what you are reading at the moment, if your answer is anything from the *Twilight* series, you may as well as pick up your coat. Like with emails, be appropriate for the adult world.

References

There are two schools of thought on this one. The first is:

References available upon request

My feeling is, why should I have to request it? You want the job, not me! If you've got people, why am I having to track them down?

The second and, I believe, more effective school of thought, is to actually give references. Ideally two professional references, from places where you've done some work experience. Give them a name, a title and an email/contact number. If you can't scare up two referees from work experience, then a teacher, personal tutor if they are willing, and perhaps a friend of your parents as a personal one.

The key thing with references is that firstly you need to cultivate those contacts to the point where they feel comfortable vouching for you and, most importantly, you let them know any time there's a possibility they'll be contacted so they aren't caught out. Remember they are putting their own reputation on the line for you: show gratitude and use their name wisely - particularly if it's a professional reference. They don't want to be fielding calls five times a week and they don't want to vouch for you and then have you suck. Earn it!

Some applications may require you to write a supporting letter. Others won't, but you may wish to take the opportunity to do so in any case. It gives you a little more creative freedom to sell to a specific need by citing very particular qualities you might possess that wouldn't otherwise come out as clearly in the CV. In essence it should be a tight, non-waffley version of your elevator pitch, but custom-made for your specific audience. Just make sure you order your letter correctly, with your address and theirs, the right date and so on. Keep it brief, show clarity of thought and explain why you believe you might be a good fit for the role in question by citing the qualities/experiences that match their requirements, but briefly.

TOP TIP: If you have a specific name that you are addressing it to, it's 'Yours sincerely', if it's Sir/Madam, it's 'Yours faithfully'.

They are the broad strokes for creating your CV. You will tinker, titivate and otherwise primp your CV to suit your purposes and it will evolve over time but for now, a neatly typed overview of your skills, abilities and experiences should be enough to get you through a few front doors. Make it confident without being cocky, assured without being complacent and sell yourself without bragging.

CASE STUDY
KEITH JOBLING

Film and music video writer and director, digital pioneer, industrial designer and the man who coined the phrase 'Madchester'. At the heart of Factory Records, his punk-inspired work ethic has given him a diverse and fascinating career that has seen him bound around the creative industries and remain at the vanguard of 'the new' working with everyone from Joy Division to Steve Coogan to John Cooper Clarke. To many he is known as Mr. Manchester, which is quite the accolade given his Geordie roots.

ME: Can you just tell me a bit about your academic past, your schooling, and fill in some of the blanks?

KJ: Okay, yeah, I lived in the north-east, between one of the worst rated towns and one of the best rated towns in the country - and I went to school in one of the worst rated towns which was the secondary modern school, but at the age of thirteen I was pushed into a grammar school. So I ended up staying in the grammar school and then I went to Newcastle Polytechnic, got on a design course that was quite tough. It was the same design course that Sir Jonathan Ives was on, the chief designer at Apple, and it was five years based around an architecture kind of model. That was in Industrial Design and I came away with a 2:1 with Honours. Instead of going straight into a design job I decided to take a year out and mess about with stuff I liked, which was film.

I ended up working in Manchester on small films and working with *Factory Records* on pop videos. I had quite a successful career working with *Factory* and various other digital artists and then we formed a digital company called *The Bootroom*. *The Bootroom* went on to win some fairly prestigious awards, stuff like Yell awards [the Oscars of the UK internet industry] and you know, for some of the digital products we did, Sex and Death CD Rom/CD [Influential album by The Durutti Column]. It was the first mixed audio/Rom type solution - it was a world first done through *Factory*. We played around with some fairly interesting stuff in the early days but it's become a bit of a slog now and that's where I'm up to. But educationally I was trained as an Industrial Designer.

ME: When you started that did you have an idea of where you wanted to be? Did you have a career path in mind?

KJ: Yeah, I was quite happy to think of myself as a product designer, in an industry, in the UK somewhere, working on whatever it would be. Some of my friends got jobs working for Baxi Boilers on the Isle of Man and designing gas fires and electric fires and stuff like that and another guy got a job in a design agency down in London and he ended up working on small-scale product design for furniture manufacturers and things like handles. The problem was the time I left college. When I joined college it looked quite an interesting lifestyle but when I left college Margaret Thatcher had wiped out 70 per cent of British industry, certainly in manufacturing that is, and decided to move to service industries, which I wasn't particularly cut out to do. So obviously I just went to film and media.

ME: When you didn't pursue the stuff that you had been training for, when you took that year, did you know you weren't ever going to go back to it in a conventional way?

KJ: Yeah absolutely, but in a way it's a similar argument about architecture, that studying architecture is the greatest education in the world for everything but architecture. Do you see what I mean? Studying as an industrial designer is primarily about problem solving, lateral thinking, understanding what the problems are really about and how people are wanting to use things rather than how they should be using them It's a kind of a set of challenges you have to overcome. There's a few good designers around: Jonny Ives is a good example of someone who has pushed it past all known boundaries, where he spends time designing how a silicon chip sits within a board. Some of the design he's doing now has never been done by an industrial designer before and it's never been done because no one ever came up and said we require this stuff, this small computer inside this tiny little thing. So in some ways the cutting edge of design has bled away from where it was all about car handles and badges and mirrors and making bits, accessories and stuff, into a much more holistic view about how stuff works and is made. So yeah, from a training point of view it's a fantastic place to come from.

ME: Okay, some of the people who will read this may not have some of the name recognition for *Factory Records* so could you just tell us a bit about that and their place in history?

KJ: Well *Factory Records* came about off the back
of the Punk movement which was a kind of do
it yourself movement, a kind of 'we're tired
of the establishment and the status quo and it
doesn't matter how bad it is, it's still better than
listening to somebody else's stuff' and some bands
that came out of that movement. There was about
ten in Manchester at that time and one of them
was *Joy Division*. The lead singer died and in
classic rock mythology his band became massive
because of his death. The record label became
much bigger than it normally would've done post
Joy Division and around the birth of *New Order*.
Although I was aware of all that going on around
Manchester, I didn't think I'd end up working for
Factory Records but I did because of the video
side. I started working with some of their newer
bands and one of them was *Happy Mondays* and we
ended up doing virtually every *Happy Mondays*
video. We did two or three *New Order* videos and
we ended up doing maybe thirty to forty videos
over a four/five year period, making one every
couple of months minimum.

ME: When you say 'we', who else was included in that?

KJ: I had a partner called Phil Shotton who was
actually from the north-east as well and he
went to the Royal College to do film and we
were working together. So we used to steal the
equipment from the Royal College of Art: he used
to book it out at the weekend and say that he
was going to clean it and practise taking it apart
and putting it back together again. But really we
didn't do any of that, we just got it for nothing
and shot film on it and then took it back the
following week and pretended we'd cleaned it and

stuff. So, it's typical kind of guerilla film-making tactics. We scammed everything we could because we were punching well above our weight in terms of some of the things we were taking on and we also got to develop a script for *Factory Records*, which was again a kind of music-orientated youth exploitation film about car thieves in Manchester, that got us maybe twenty meetings in London with anybody and everybody. We met Puttnam [Lord David Puttnam - Oscar-winning producer and former CEO of Columbia Pictures], we won the Goldcrest Prize for one of the short films we did at the Royal College and we won a Silver Hugo at the Chicago Film Festival for the final year film that Phil did and I wrote that and was Producer/ Assistant Director on. So things like that.

I was working and he was at college for the first, sort of, year and a half of that but it kind of worked out. So when he finished we just carried on working and formed a business called Bailey Brothers and also formed another business called Screen Intelligence and we worked producing and directing pop videos. We did some documentaries for Granada, 'cause obviously Wilson [Tony Wilson - owner of Factory Records] worked for Granada. We did some TV programmes like *The Other Side of Midnight*, the Leeds Film Festival which was like a double bill thing; we did something on Clive Barker as a special and we did a few other bits and pieces that were music related for *The Other Side of Midnight*, also doing film reviews as well which was just bonkers.

Anyway, when *Factory* crashed and burned during a very tough period for the music industry, we'd already formed a digital company with Wilson.

I'd kind of given up chasing the British film
industry around because we'd done so many
meetings, we'd met everybody and, after about
a three or four year period of working on the
feature script, I'd worked out there was anybody
really there. It wasn't a real industry and it was
a minute cottage industry pretending it was an
industry and virtually everything that really
happened happened because it was an American
based company spending money in the UK and that
was all done through a very, very tight circle.
Even though we got to meet people like Sandy
Leiberson who had been Head of Production for
20th Century Fox, his first film as producer had
been the Nic Roeg film with Mick Jagger in,
Performance. He had a track record the length
of his arm and he'd just done a Northern comedy
here and he wanted to do our film, which was
called *The Mad F*ckers*, or *TMF* for short. Really
it was just an exploitation movie - a couple of
kids in a car who assume they are being chased,
but they're not really, and a bunch of gangsters
who are having loads of problems because the car
that was stolen had a clue to where some missing
money was. So, it's a pretty typical low-key
exploitation movie and it was £4 million and we
had James Bond's stunt director on board and we
had Graham Brown as cinematographer on board;
we had about half of the money stumped up but we
couldn't attach a star. Albert Finney said he'd do
it if we couldn't get anybody else but he thought
he was too old for the role and he kind of was.
Gabriel Byrne said he'd do it if they could raise
the money and at the time they couldn't; they
couldn't raise the money on Gabriel Byrne, that's
what they said! They wanted Gary Oldman, and

to be honest he was completely wrong for us, he was too young, too raw. At the time, it just didn't make sense and we ended up going round in circles and I just got incredibly bored with the idea that these people were ever going to pull it off and that we would get to direct it. John McKenzie, who's a Scots director who'd shot a lot of stuff with Billy Connolly, came on board as director and we were just going to be kind of riding shotgun but the money just never turned up really.

It was just make-believe and I got very bored with the whole thing. It was just a big lie and I left Phil to get on with it and he was convinced that once he was full director of the project he could get rid of John and he'd take over and it'd all get made.

About two years later, after we set up *The Bootroom* as a digital company and we'd done the world's first mixed audio format, like Red Book/Blue Book CD Rom and it was in the *Guinness Book of Records...* We had four or five commissions out and I was still doing pop promos as an individual; I did some quite interesting stuff by myself and carried on with the digital company. We did all sorts of interesting big projects and also lots of interesting small projects. We did *Government Office Northwest* which was a big Oracle development and we were the only company in the country to pull off a regional, never mind a national, version of what was a very complex database solution for what was effectively monitoring European funding.

ME: Did you kind of pivot when you saw there wasn't a route to market with the film thing and then move towards the digital? Was it the result of a plan or did you just see the way things were going?

KJ: A bit of both I suppose. What happened was, when we were making *The World in Motion*, the England World Cup video, we got inundated with offers to go and work in advertising. For whatever reason, looking back on it you could argue it was just a really stupid idea; we didn't want to have to do advertising to 'earn the right' to make films. This career path where you had to earn your stripes, pay your dues, work hard in advertising for two years, build a career as a big advertising name before someone would let you make a movie. I just thought 'F*ck off!' Why would we have to do that? We can just make our own movie for £100,000 and tell these w*nkers in London to f*ck off, 'cause we don't need £4 million to make a car chase movie, we just need a £100,000 and do it all ourselves in a kind of guerrilla style. Wilson was very keen to do that. It had even got to the point where someone was offering him £250,000 for the soundtrack package. They would do it and make their money out of distribution and we would get a share of that after they'd made their £250K back and we'd sign the bands up to it. That was part of the nature of those kinds of films; it was exploitation on every level, so it would've been some bands we'd stuck together and some bands would break through and look cool because they were attached to this film.

So, that was just about on the cusp of working when *Factory* started going under, or not going under but struggling, and it looked obvious that we weren't going to be able to raise the money in that period. I just thought, well, the chances of it happening are slim and I could spend the rest of my life cycling round this empty goldfish bowl full of w*nkers going on about film when really it's never going to happen. So the digital stuff, 'cause I was trained as a designer and I had lot of skills overlapping what I could do in terms of film, video and writing, I just sort of got stuck in doing stuff on computers and at the time it was very raw still. CDs were like the new big thing. People had numbers for email addresses and it was all very new and there weren't many people around doing it and we kind of ploughed our own furrow and in some ways all I wanted to do was not have to listen to some idiot that was telling us that because they worked for an advertising agency in London they knew better than me how about how this should look or what this should be and then I'd have to do it because that's the job.

ME: Would you say that your entrepreneurial spirit or get-up-and-go or whatever you want to call it was fuelled by ambition or was it just an unwillingness to listen to other people?

KJ: [Laughs]. Probably a bit of both. Again you have to remember we were formed in the white hot heat of punk, which was very anti-establishment, very 'everybody who's currently doing stuff is a w*nker' and they were boring, 'get out of the way, make some room for the kids'; that was us. So as you kind of moved through that, the account execs would sit us down and say, 'we don't really understand what your problem is. We're offering you sixty grand to do a Mars Bar advert. It'll take you two f*cking days and John Barnes wants to do it with you; he wants to do the Mars Bar advert

with you. If you don't want to do it, fine, don't do
it, but someone is going to do it exactly how we're
going to do it anyway and John Barnes will end up
saying what happened to the guys I worked with
on the video and they'll say oh, they got more
money elsewhere and so, just do it, just take the
money and do it!' And it was that kind of smooth,
kind of slippery, sign your life away here with
blood on this piece of paper, you'll be rich and
everything will work. It just didn't smell right.
It stunk, in terms of who I was and where I was at
that point in the world. It just didn't make sense
to us. I just thought 'f*ck off, there's absolutely
no way I'm doing that'. When they said, 'what's
wrong with advertising?' I just said, 'Don't you
think there's enough crap in the world, and do you
think selling more and more crap forever is a great
reason to be on this planet?' and the guy looked
at us and just went, 'you're f*cking nuts. Seeya.'
And that was that, literally. He just couldn't see
my point of view that this idea, this crass idea
of making money out of selling cigarettes to kids
which is why Puttnam on that documentary at the
end was virtually in tears because he didn't realise
what he was doing when he was making Silk Cut
adverts; he thought he was making art. I just
thought that was incredibly naive. If you could get
a decent wage working on something you thought
was valid, something valuable and useful, maybe I
wouldn't have been so against it. But it wasn't, it
was just sh*t, it was all just crap and why would
I want to do that? Why would I want to sell kids
more sugar, you know?

It was sad, I thought. It was more fun cutting
your own swathe through the embryonic digital
industry, doing loads of stuff, making a sort of

decent living and working on the birth of the
computer on the planet in Manchester. We just
did some mad, crazy and valuable stuff. Partly
because of Wilson and what he was plugged into
and he just used to bring us in and say, 'can we
do this?' and 'we've got this budget - what do
you think?' That was the big difference really;
that was what spoiled it for me, 'cause Wilson
would turn up and say, 'here's the single, that's
the budget, there's the cheque, can you get the
finished video to *Top of the Pops* three weeks on
Wednesday?' That was it, literally. He might go
away at that point and we might never see him
for the three weeks, and we'd finish the video
and it would be broadcast on *Top of the Pops*, go
out live without anybody, the band, the manager,
Wilson, *Factory*, nothing seeing it. It was just
complete trust, 'can you do that? Great - thanks
guys,' and if we rang up and said there was a
problem with the budget, he'd just say, 'what's
the damage, okay we'll sort it out, or we'll put it
on the next one' or whatever. D'you know what
I mean? It was always just managed beautifully,
never not paid, never argued over money, he
said what the budget was; if we said it was a bit
small he'd go away and see if he could get more
and if he couldn't we'd just change our idea so
we could do it. It was just like a really proper
holistic relationship from a creative point of
view. You knew you could be stupid and get away
with it but you didn't really want to do that,
you wanted to do something that people would
be happy with, so the band would say, 'yeah we
really liked that' and the record company would
be 'yeah it's great'.

ME: Looking back now, you took a fairly zigzag route and I'm sure there's things you might have done a little differently in retrospect but is there anything that you're particularly proud of, or that you're pleased you took a risk on?

KJ: Career-wise, I think in a way I always wanted to work in film and video and in the visual medium. At school I was a painter, I used to paint - I was dragged around everywhere for being good at painting and art and every time I thought about wanting to do something in that space I just realised how difficult it is to make a living being a painter. So what other kind of things can you do career-wise? What can you do that allows you to use that urge to create but that you can make a living out of? So in a way the problem you've got is that the world just kind of happens with or without you and you either tag along and try and fit in and make sense of how good you are at what you do with the rest of the world, or the bit you're adjoined to, or you just drop out completely and just hope that at some point it will all make sense. I suppose my worry always was that if you just drop out completely to become a painter you could be Van Gogh, who creates this amazing stuff but nobody cares; he dies miserably in poverty, and everybody around him, he's made everyone who knows him's lives a misery because of his struggle and the fact that nobody could help him. Then 200 years later his stuff is some of the most expensive stuff in the history of ever. That's part of the worry, that in some ways your career is more of a strategic kind of approach of making sense of the skill sets you've got and what you can do with them in what is effectively a marketplace for those skill sets.

ME: So what recommendations would you offer young people coming through now, not necessarily those trying to access a career in your industry? But reflecting on your own do-it-yourself, 'punk' sensibility, how would you encourage people to approach it?

KJ: I think the world has changed beyond recognition. When I was getting career advice people would get a job down the mine for life. They would literally join the mine as an electrician and assumed they'd retire with a gold watch as a manager, as a respected miner and they would've spent half their life down a black hole digging in coal. That's what people did for a living. People fought for those jobs. My Dad used to say, 'the last thing you want to do is go down the pit, that'd just be a waste of everything you've got.' All the big industries have gone now and the bits that haven't are going to end up being done by robots anyway, so really if I was starting again now I'd try and choose some sort of multi-disciplined course where you can learn lots of different types of skills. Whether it be creative or technical ones, and the clever kind of thing is try and combine both so you've got creative skills and some technical skills. When you have a skill see if it's obsolete. Is the skill you've got today still as valuable as it was a month ago and is it valuable enough to do what you need to do next month? So you're just on this constant treadmill of picking up new ideas and skills and attitudes to doing stuff and understanding clever ways of doing it.

It's a competitive environment and most people don't assume they're going to have a job for more than ten years in any one given area before they have to move on or change completely. People are making a living by having three different jobs. You know, they're doing *Uber* at night, they're working in a coffee shop in the morning and then doing something else in their spare time to try and get a career in the area they really want. That's a fairly common model in this day and age, where people have the aspiration to do one thing but it's going to be really tough to pull that off, so in the meantime they do other stuff whilst they're trying. It's the LA model where everyone who works in a restaurant is either an actor, a writer, a director or a producer, all working as waiters in places they think they may see people who can help them. It's that thing of clinging to the top of that very steep hill of where you want to be and the majority of people struggle to get halfway up that hill but that's often more than enough in terms of being able to make a decent life for yourself. You could argue that it's got easier in some ways with technology but you could also argue it's much harder; technology has made that playing field much flatter and therefore what skill and talent you have got, you've got to make more of it than the guy next door who's trying to compete.

ME: Thank you.

9

MEET AND GREET

'Daniel Goleman has proven that two-thirds of the
success in business is based upon our Emotional
Intelligence as opposed to our IQ or our level of
experience. As we look for the next crop of future
CEOs, maybe it's time for America's corporations to
start interviewing grads from the psychology master's
programs rather than the MBA programs.'

Chip Conley

What does the above quote mean? Well rather than me try and dissect all of Daniel Goleman's work I would simply refer you to read the two equally excellent books - *Social Intelligence: The New Science of Human Relationships* and *Emotional Intelligence & Working with Emotional Intelligence*. If you don't have time for that in amongst all the other things on your plate then of course I entirely understand, but what both books explore in a really fascinating way is the science behind how we interact with one another, how we process first impressions and how our brain chemistry is actually physically altered on a cellular level with every meeting. It's how we process everything from a perceived threat to a potential love interest. Why is this important? When you understand how and why people respond to you in a certain way then you are much better placed to effectively alter and manipulate your behaviour to suit your audience.

What I'm suggesting here is not necessarily as evil and moustache-twisty as it sounds. This isn't about trying to hoodwink people; this is about trying to adapt your behaviour to encourage greater levels of neural handshaking between you and the person you are speaking to. This is how every social interaction works to some degree or another. If you walk into a shop and speak to a cashier the nature of your interaction and relationship is very clear: you are the customer, they are the cashier. Your interaction will go down very predictable lines because both of you inherently understand the roles you are there to play. This is reflected in your body language, amount of eye contact, the words you choose. It is not necessarily formal but nor is it highly personalised. I'm sure you will have had occasion to be more familiar and try and joke with them; they too will adopt a less formal approach and it becomes instantly more human and natural but equally you will have had occasions when they will just look at you weirdly for breaking character, as it were. By switching roles and being less the customer and more social, sometimes they don't react well, maybe they're not in the mood, maybe it's caught them off guard, or they're having a bad day or maybe they just don't like you for whatever reason. After that sort of rebuffal you will resort to type and go back to customer mode. All of which is a very long-winded way of saying that in everyday life you are unwittingly practising a series of approaches: rebalancing and counter-reactions that hinge on reading social cues and innate emotional intelligence to dictate how you interact with others, to manipulate them to make them like you, help you, elicit a laugh, make a good impression and so on.

When I was younger I pretended that I never much cared what anyone thought of me, hence wearing odd clothes that I found in the school's costume department. Even as a youngish/older man who had been working in recruitment for quite some time (so should have known better), I still exercised a rather smug idiocy when it came to my personal life. My wife is always keen to remind me that prior to meeting her Mum for the first time my attitude was, 'I don't care what she thinks, I'm not going out with her.' Which was not just naive but also incredibly rude and dismissive - obviously there's something terribly wrong with me, but I like to think that I've grown up since then. However this kind of thing is much more likely to happen in less emotionally intelligent people and unfortunately EI is something you tend to develop more as you get older. As a teenager I was, and indeed most of my peers were, pretty self-involved. Yes, of course we cared about our friends and family and so on but empathy and understanding weren't necessarily the first tools we'd resort to when required - an issue which I'm sure will be familiar to you. Processing emotion in an adult way is by its very nature something you learn as you mature into an adult. By making yourself aware of not just the social conventions but also the social expectations, you are much better equipped to deal with people, to ensure you make a good first impression, interview well, fit into differing environments and can operate as part of a team.

The lessons and suggestions I am promoting below are as relevant for you today, interviewing for your first job or work experience or internship, as they will be for a seasoned veteran going for one last job before retirement. Yes it is weighted towards interviewing for a role but whenever you are in a situation where you are asked to sell yourself or talk about yourself and what you can offer, what follows is a solid foundation to work from, no matter what the specific circumstances and no matter where you are on your journey.

First impressions count

Not for nothing do people keep reminding you of this. It's true. Absolutely, incontrovertibly true, and those first impressions happen a hell of a lot quicker than you imagine. What do you think? The first five minutes? Three minutes? Try a tenth of a second. Yup. Say it with me if it helps, 'a tenth of a second'. That's not far off a single frame of a TV programme. According to a study conducted at Princeton by psychologists Janine Willis and Alexander Todorov, they reveal you will form an impression of a stranger from their face in under a tenth of a second, and that longer exposures don't significantly alter that initial impression; in fact you will spend that remaining time looking for evidence to back up your initial impression. (Their research is presented in their article '"First Impressions,' in the July 2006 issue of *Psychological Science*.)

Subconsciously you will be making assessments of a range of things from attractiveness, likeability, competence, trustworthiness and aggression. This is at its most basic level the kind of 'fight or flight' thinking that we've evolved. We make snap judgements on people's faces not to be mean but in essence to establish whether we believe them to be a threat. There is evidence of this everywhere - for instance in the court rooms, where one would hope that fair play and rule of law should be the deciding factors, when it comes to sentencing, those with more 'mature' faces as opposed to those with 'baby' faces are more likely to be handed down much sterner sentences. Like it or not, we are, as a people, still governed by the aesthetic and we can rail against how unfair that is or we can accept it as a part of life and do what we can to use that understanding to our advantage.

Now obviously you can't change your face - glasses, beards and balaclavas remain an option but in broad strokes you cannot change your appearance drastically on an elemental level, although there are certainly steps you can take to make the best of yourself. What you do have more control over is your body language, eye contact, the frequency of your smile, the words you choose, and the manner in which you conduct yourself.

If we break this down into more digestible pieces and at the risk of repeating some of what we covered in the informational interviewing section, let's consider best practice activities to make a good first impression.

Appearance

As covered previously, assuming you are interviewing for a role that isn't focused on fashion or the creative arts, then you are not there to make brash statements about your unique sense of style. You are there to offer comfort and reassurance that you can do the job you are interviewing for and even in quasi creative places like the media they are looking for a level of professionalism. The quickest and easiest way to demonstrate that you are both taking the interview seriously and understand what professionalism means is to dress the part.

You are never going to offend anyone by looking smart. Even if they are dressed in a more relaxed way, you can simply adjust your attitude and language so it more accurately mirrors the tone they set, to reassure them that you are not 'too formal' for the business. So for one and all that means washing your hair, brushing it away from your face - as covered previously, a tenth of a second is the processing time required to make a judgement: that is done through micro reactions to facial cues, much harder to do if your face is obscured by a fringe. If you have long hair, tie it up. If you are thinking of sporting a wispy moustache or beard I would urge caution.

So shave, wash and preen. Not only does this make you look more polished and professional but, given your relative youth, the 'baby' face dynamic comes into play, making you look altogether more trustworthy which is what you are striving for. If you have a suit then of course do wear it. If however you have a suit that is a hand-me- down from your mum or dad and it doesn't quite fit you, then don't. A poorly fitting suit is much worse than smart trousers and a shirt and tie or equivalent. Details do count, so polished shoes, clipped and cleaned finger nails, clothes that have been ironed, etc are all easy little things that are within your control.

I wouldn't presume to tell you or anyone how to dress or the amount of make up/hair wax and so on to wear, but sometimes less is more. This isn't war paint on a night out; this needs to be professional and demure. You're after a job, not a romantic encounter. You must tailor your appearance to meet the expectations of your audience.

Why is this so important? In an interview situation there are lots of unknowns - you don't know exactly what they will ask, how they will react to you, what precisely they are looking for - there are a lot of unknown factors that are beyond your control, but making sure your shoes are clean, your clothes ironed and that you look the part are factors that are entirely within your control. By ensuring you get the little things right you a) don't have to be self conscious and worry that you look out of place, b) can focus on the job at hand and c) ensure you are not struggling for the rest of the interview to overcome their first impression of you.

If you are a smoker - do not under any circumstances be tempted to smoke prior to getting ready for your meeting. As smoking has become less and less commonplace the smell is considerably more conspicuous and off-putting for many people. Moreover, smokers take more frequent breaks throughout the day and are generally considered less productive for that. Also, don't chew gum: it just looks rude; no one wants to listen to you masticate hour old chuddy.

The handshake

Given all the literature and informational *YouTube* videos and the general understanding that exists within the collective consciousness, I'm always surprised by how frequent and unpleasant it is when one is presented with a wet-fish rather than a solid handshake.

A handshake should be firm, last for no more than three shakes and include the whole hand. Firm, in so much as there's something to grip on to, not that you are trying to prove anything and crush their hand. It should also be presented straight forward - offering them the hand with palm down suggests you are trying to establish dominance, palm up is submissive. Never double hand it; never put one hand over the top of theirs once the shake is 'on' unless you are a Vegas mobster. It's a power assertion move but is over-familiar and inappropriate for a business setting. However, if they do it to you at the end, that's actually quite a good thing.

Do not, as some people like to do, present just your fingers, almost like you're the Pope and are waiting for the person to kiss the papal seal. Do not present a wet limp hand - it's most off-putting and people will draw conclusions that you are equally wet and uninspiring based on that interaction.

Body language

One could write a whole book about this; indeed many have. Personally I couldn't because it's not really my field of expertise but there are certainly a few little tips and general good practice things that you can work into your routine.

OPEN - this is the key: don't fold your arms It looks either sulky or that you are trying to self-soothe. Moreover it suggests a kind of 'go on then impress me' type attitude. You are physically installing a barrier between you and the interviewer. Same goes for demonstrative leg crossing.

FIDGETING - don't fiddle, tap your feet or fingers, play with a pen, twitch or move around in your seat. It can be extraordinarily off-putting to someone interviewing you and once they start to tune into it, it will be all they can focus on. Same goes for shuffling.

GOOD POSTURE - slouching: don't do it. At best it looks too relaxed; at worse it looks disinterested and rude. Sit up straight: it makes you look engaged with them, with the interview, and will give them a much greater sense that you are not only taking this seriously but that this will translate into your professional life.

EYE CONTACT - you want to find a balance between making eye contact and staring people down. If you look away or down constantly it looks like you're being evasive or don't have confidence in what you are saying. Also if you don't make eye contact it can look like you're not fully engaged and don't have much interest in what they might be saying to you.

MIRRORING - it is a proven trick that people feel more warmly disposed to others when that person's body language mirrors their own. It tacitly suggests a level of comfort and ease which is good but also subconsciously suggests to them that you share similar views, hold similar opinions and are on the same wavelength. If you look at couples you will often see their body language mirrors one another. Obviously try to be subtle but mirroring does help establish trust and confidence.

THE LEAN - by leaning slightly forwards in your chair you demonstrate your interest in what that person has to say. It makes you look more energetic, more proactive. Lean too far and it makes you look like you have issues with your hearing or are trying to intimidate the other person. Subtlety, like mirroring, is the order of the day.

First impressions checklist -

- Project confidence: smile, establish eye contact and use a firm handshake.

- Posture counts: Sit up straight yet comfortably; be aware of nervous gestures such as foot-tapping.

- Be attentive: don't stare, but maintain good eye contact, while addressing all aspects of an interviewer's questions.

- Respect their space: do not place anything on their desk.

- Manage reactions: facial expressions provide clues to your feelings. Manage how you react, and project a positive image.

- Pay attention to non-verbal communication.

Reading the room

Often you will be meeting more than one person at a time, perhaps a line manager and someone from HR (Human Resources) or a similar combination. Often, in this instance, one person will lead the interview and the second one may not be as actively engaged - instead taking notes in the background. From that dynamic it is very easy to make judgements (often incorrectly) about where the power lies. In this situation you have two people - a decision maker and an influencer. By making a judgement about where the power rests and focusing your attention on the decision maker you risk alienating the influencer.

Imagine a situation socially where you are trying to woo (yeah, I know) a boy or a girl who is out with a friend. The last thing you want to do is annoy the friend. You want them on side so they'll talk you up to their friend - an interview is no different. Even if the influencer isn't talking much you need to try and bring them into the conversation at least with your body language and eye contact. If someone asks you a question both parties need to feel engaged when you answer, for three very clear reasons -

1) You don't know how much influence the influencer has.

2) If they are not engaged they might just drift off and have no opinion of you. Spending an hour with you and coming away with no feelings one way or another is not a good sign.

3) They may feel that you are arrogant and aloof, and dismissive of them - no one likes to feel marginalised.

So, what I mean by reading the room is trying to quickly gauge what dynamics are in play, understanding what's required of you and adapting quickly to often changing situations. Nowhere is this more necessary than in a group interview situation. This is quite a common way to do things in certain industries, specifically in industries or roles that require you to work as part of a team or in a collaborative way.

Group interviews

Firstly, if you understand what the role requires you should be able to modulate your behaviour to suit their requirements. That is, if the role requires you to work well as part of a team, you standing there talking over other people, shouting the loudest, will certainly get you noticed but not in a good way; equally, being a shrinking violet and saying nothing to avoid seeming too pushy will also not do you any favours.

Often in this situation they will set you some sort of group task or activity and then monitor how you interact with others. Whether you solve the task or problem is almost immaterial, it's much more about how you have performed in the group dynamic. You want to be heard, but not at the expense of putting people down or winding them up by talking over them. People wrongly assume that being the alpha in this environment is everything, but actually being a shrewd number 2 who can paddle in the slipstream behind the disruptive noisemaker and help bridge the gap between the loudmouth and the more reserved ones will be a much more useful addition to a team than a know-it-all. Sometimes not beating your chest is the easiest way to get noticed.

In these team tasks where you may be asked to perform or to solve a problem it is incumbent upon you to put yourself forward to be noticed, ask questions, be collaborative but not dictatorial, encourage others to speak up. If you can slot yourself into that facilitator role that is much more likely to mark you out as being a potential leader; the best managers are the ones that can get the best out of an employee and rarely, if ever, does this involve being able to shout the loudest. Any company that is hiring will always want to engage with ambitious people who at least have the potential to move forward and grow with the business.

All of which comes back to reading the room. Think about what is expected of you, try and get a read on the people you are dealing with. In any group of six or eight you will find at least one trying to shout the odds; don't worry about them - like the big, bad wolf, they soon run out of puff. You will find a couple who are utterly passive and say nothing and you will find the middlers. Humans are pack animals; it's in our nature - hell, it's hardwired into our DNA - that we do better as a group than as an individual. By making sensible suggestions and asking questions of the more passive ones you start to gently direct the action and people will line up behind you. Partly they will do so as a reaction to the most vocal and irritating one in the room and partly because they will be relieved that someone has put themselves forward and taken the heat off them. This is a much better way to get noticed than to scream 'listen to me!' Let the alpha blow themselves out (in my experience it will most likely be a bloke - to the constant shame of my gender) or get distracted locking horns with someone else.

Group interview checklist -

- Depends on nature of job.

- If the job allows any chance of promotion to a supervisory role, then you need to be vocal, promote yourself to the forefront, and demonstrate leadership without bullying/talking over people (eg if team-based, be firm but supportive, collaborate but guide).

- If it's a team-building exercise, then you need to make an impact, but don't promote yourself at the expense of others.

Some thoughts about university interviews

Obviously not everyone will have to interview for a place at university but many of you will and, whilst the bulk of what I've said above and later will hold true for a university interview, there are obviously some specific issues to consider. In both interview situations you will be judged on your potential but even more so in a university interview; they don't need you to make an immediate impact, as they might in a job, but they will want you to have the ability to meet the challenges of the course and the ambition and interest to thrive. In universities yes, of course they want the brightest and the best, but equally they are more forgiving than a job where there's only one place to be filled. Focus on your interest in the subject, capacity for independent thought, and rely on examples of your commitment to a potential future career or your demonstrable enthusiasm for the course and what you've done outside the norm to try and secure your place.

- Interviews can range from an 'exam out loud' (expect this from Oxbridge) to an informal chat designed to encourage you to choose that course.

- They can last anything from ten minutes to an hour and are usually, though not always, conducted by one interviewer.

- They will vary depending on the subject you're applying to study – eg English students may have to discuss a poem, while maths applicants might be asked to solve an equation.

- Whatever the format of your interview, remember you're there for answers too. It's a conversation after all, not just you fielding questions. They want you to respond to what they're asking of course but they also want you to contribute.

- Breathe! This is a chance to talk about a subject you and the interviewer have a shared interest in.

- As with career interviews, having a few sensible, well thought through questions will impress your interviewer just as much as good answers.

What are interviewers/tutors looking for?

- Enthusiasm. They want passion and excitement.

- An understanding of your reasons for wanting to study that particular subject.

- Certainty that you're aware of what the course involves and what the career options are.

- Ability to present your ideas and arguments well, demonstrating your ability to think. Do not regurgitate second-hand opinion but actually think independently.

- Knowledge you have gained from any extra-curricular work you have done, and how you have applied that to your current thinking, whether that's work experience, a gap year, research - whatever it may be. They will partly want to test your commitment and ensure it's not just box-ticking but will also want to make sure you're not wildly exaggerating your claims.

- Assurance that you can handle the rigours and stress of the course and will last. No one wants to waste a space on someone who doesn't look like they'll make it to the end.

- A willingness to engage with new ideas, be open to debate - willing to be wrong or argue that you're right, that you can read beyond and outside the narrow limitations of a course curriculum and come with fresh ideas.

University interview checklist

- Research the course.
- Clearly articulate what and why you are attracted to the subject.
- Think about where you want it to take you longer term.
- Make sure you can back up any claims you make.
- Have your own thoughts.
- Have good questions.

Research

What? Research? Really? Well, this is new. Obviously, yes, you need to do your homework. It's like I said before: with so many unknown variables, it's paramount that you try to nail down the easy low hanging fruit that you do have control of.

RESEARCH THE ROLE - most businesses will have generated something, some paperwork that states the aims and objectives of the role, reporting lines, team size and so on. The more you can learn about the nature of what they are looking for, the easier it is to sell to that need. Have a look at people with the same job title online, find out what they do, get some different perspectives. People on Linked In, for instance, pretty much put their CVs up on line. If you can look through someone's CV you can get a much more accurate understanding of what a role entails and, crucially, what success might look like for someone in that role.

Think about anyone in your extended and ever-growing network that may have done the role and ask what insights they could offer. I remember way back when, before I interviewed for my first role in recruitment, that I had this impression of lovely, softly-softly people just working their cottons off to try and get other people that dream job. I spoke to a friend of mine who had worked in recruitment way back in his past and he told me that quite the opposite was true and it's a hard-nosed sales role with lots of cold calling and soft skills needed. It came as quite a revelation. It seems obvious now, but as an outsider, I didn't get it. That was what helped me get the job, as it turned my preparation on its head and changed my focus.

If you have got the role via a recruitment consultant or agency they should be able to give you all that you need in the way of background on the role, but if you have applied directly to the company hiring, go back to the advert and study that again. There is no harm in asking whoever it is that you are liaising with to set up the meeting whether a job description has been generated or whether they could give you something of a steer towards what the interview will cover, or any background on the role that would be useful for you to know as you go through your research and preparation.

RESEARCH THE BUSINESS - as with informational interviewing, don't be lazy about it. There will be a lot of information out there somewhere, even just on their website or in trade mags-or local news. Whatever it might be, the better you understand a company, the better quality questions you can ask, the more you can tailor your approach to match their culture and so on. If you know they are on the verge of a takeover or relocating to a new building or have appointed a new MD or anything else like that, it can spark a fresh wave of conversation, which can help you better understand the business and help you in your decision about whether it's the right role for you.

RESEARCH THE COURSE AND THE UNIVERSITY - if it is an academic interview, know the subject matter, understand the course requirements and what will be covered, know about the university and its reputation, the lecturers and so on.

SIDEBAR

It's easy to lose sight of the fact that an interview is a two way street. Yes you need to impress them, but if you are good then they are going to want you too, and you need to make sure that this role makes sense for your longer term prospects. All of this means the more research you do, the better the questions you ask, the better informed your decision will be.

RESEARCH THE PEOPLE YOU ARE MEETING - the easiest way is to ask whoever it is that is setting up the meeting if they could give you an idea of the format of the meeting: if it's a very formal Q&A session that tells you something about the person you'll be meeting, if they pitch it as an informal chat that too tells you something. If you're going via an agency they should be able to give you more detail on the people and personalities, certain hot buttons they are looking for, things that they don't want to see. If you don't have that advantage, then go and spy on them on Linked In. You may wish to do it anonymously as people can see who's been looking at their profile, but there's no shame in researching and it may actually count in your favour.

When you are remotely checking them out, take the time to go through their experience, look for things that are noteworthy or interesting, look for certain commonalities, be it where you're from, interests, or schooling. Anything you can glean from their profile will give you a slight edge, a way to open the door potentially to a more human interaction, which in turn breeds trust and goodwill. It could be as easy as saying, 'I noticed on your LinkedIn profile you went to X, did X, are interested in X; so am I,' or 'this is something I was keen to look into in the future'. Something soft like that can help establish your interest and diligence, and, ideally, them seeing something of themselves in you can be very appealing to a lot of managers.

RESEARCH YOUR CV - sounds dumb, right? It's your CV. Of course you know it! You wrote the thing, these are your experiences. The trouble is most of us write the CV, play with it to appeal to a specific audience, bringing certain skills or experiences to the foreground, and by the time we've done that a few times it's hard to remember what we kept in, what we left off and so on. The interviewer, however, has no such confusion and indeed will have spent the ten minutes before coming in to meet you going through it with a fine toothcomb. Don't get tripped up on your CV! Take the time to put the CV up against the job description or advert - really analyse what they are looking for and think about what you've done, what you can offer, and how that maps on to their requirements. Then take those answers and turn them into demonstrable, anecdotal examples of experiences that the interviewer will be interested to hear about.

That's your research done. Now it's just everything else...

Practise

'Practise what?' I hear you ask. Everything! People are, generally speaking, a fairly circumspect lot. We find talking about ourselves mildly embarrassing and suggesting we are good at something positively mortifying. That is why it is essential, particularly at this stage of your career, to practise as much as possible. Your school should be organising mock interviews for you in any case but don't rely on them. Get your parents, your friends' parents, your parents' friends, to give you ten minutes, twenty minutes, to practise. The more comfortable you get discussing you, who you are, what you can offer, what your ambitions are, the easier you'll find it. It will be uncomfortable and awkward and clunky initially but it's an entirely new skill you're learning and it takes a while to get good. You don't want to pre-prepare answers because you don't know specifically what they may ask, and trying to shoehorn an answer into a space that it doesn't quite belong in isn't great, plus it always sounds wooden and inauthentic. But if you can practise the art of selling yourself in a subtle and useful way, if you can remember to answer the question you've been asked (as opposed to the one you had a really good answer for), you will do well.

Weirdly, when it comes to practising, it's the people you are most comfortable with that will be the hardest to practise with - talking about your strengths and experience with your parents or a friend will be excruciatingly embarrassing; you will be self-conscious and awkward and tempted to make jokes to cover how self-conscious you are. It is for precisely this reason that you should practise with them: after that, talking to a stranger will be a doddle.

The importance of this is for you to start to feel relaxed about selling yourself. Once you relax and it becomes more natural some of those nerves will disappear and then it will flow more,which in turn will make you feel increasingly relaxed, and so on and so on. Knowing your CV and rehearsing different scenarios can massively boost your overall performance as it will be more naturalistic, and when you can promote the idea of your own confidence in your abilities this will give the person you are speaking to confidence in what you are saying.

What you are aiming for in both your practice and in real interviews is to project a relaxed, articulate and capable individual: sure of your abilities and confident, but never crossing over into arrogance. Don't ever try to wing it or lay claim to talents or experiences you don't have: this is the quickest way to become unstuck. If, for example, they are asking about your experience of X, think about what you *have* had experiences of and how that might be transferable into this new arena. It's honest, considered, and, as long as you keep your head and can think fast, shows logical, problem solving skills.

The reality is you would not be sitting in front of the person interviewing you if they did not believe there was at least a possibility that you could do the job. They have seen your CV; they know what you have and haven't done. Your experience will not have changed simply by being in the room, so when they ask leading questions it's not an attempt to trip you up but rather to explore whether you have the capacity for lateral thought. Hence, never lie, but rather use the experiences you've had to reassure them you have the ability to do a set task even if you've not done exactly the same thing previously.

Active listening

Someone once said in a film, 'there are two types of people, those who listen and those who wait to talk'. In an interview situation, and arguably in life generally, you should strive to be the latter. There are so many benefits to actively listening, but before we get into them, perhaps I should explain what I mean.

ACTIVE LISTENING - a communication technique popular with trainers, counsellors, therapists and within arbitration/conflict resolution. The technique ensures that the listener fully concentrates, understands, responds and then recalls what has been said. This is as opposed to reflective listening where the listener repeats back to the speaker what they have just heard to confirm understanding.

For your purposes, because we're obviously not going to skill you up as therapists in this book, the important thing is to understand that there is a difference between hearing and listening. You can't help what you hear but listening is a studied practice requiring concentration.

Once you are fully engaged in what the speaker, or in this case interviewer, is saying or asking then you give yourself a much better opportunity to speak to a specific need and, crucially, at the right point. How many of us have been in a conversation, thought it was going one way and started to answer, before we knew what was really going to be said? I'd guess all of us. It goes back to the two ears one mouth philosophy. By employing active listening you are much more likely to pick up on the non-verbal cues that the speaker will be throwing out, letting you know when they are finished, acknowledging understanding, sympathy, and so on. If you are simply waiting to give them an answer you think they might be interested in, not only will you not pick up on all these little cues they are giving you, you will give them information they haven't asked for, and possibly have no need for, and you will look rude.

The STAR technique for answering behavioural questions

This is a handy mnemonic that, whilst formulaic, can help you run through a mental checklist to make sure you answer every element of a question. When you are nervous, as you will likely be in an interview situation, having some foundations to underpin the looser chat may just give you the confidence to loosen up a little and be more natural, which is where techniques like this can be handy.

Any question that an interviewer asks serves the purpose of trying to see whether your skill and experience could work for the role you are discussing. Using this framework to answer helps ensure you don't leave anything out and has a thorough and logical methodology.

S - situation - detail the background, give them some context: what, when, where etc.

T - task - what did you need to do? What was the challenge? Why and so on?

A - action - what did you personally do? What specific action did you take and how did you do it?

R - result - what was the outcome? Quantify it: savings, recognition, benefits, accomplishments and so on.

Good question

As touched on earlier, a good well thought out question can do a variety of wonderful things. You can demonstrate your commitment to the process: that is, you're not phoning it in - this is something you've sat down and taken the time to think about. This is not just flattering to them but reassuring and it paints you in a positive light. It can open up new areas of discussion that will further your understanding of the role and company and may give you a new opportunity to sell yourself to them. Most, if not all interviews, will end with "Do you have any questions?" So, bring a list.

SIDEBAR

When I say list, don't bring a vast pad and go through them all. They ask the question as a bit of courtesy and don't want to spend another hour detailing holiday entitlement, length of time of breaks, etc. Keep it high level and never discuss money in a first interview unless expressly brought up by them. If you are going to take notes, do ask whether it is okay to do so: no one wants to spend their time talking to the top of your head as you scribble away.

EXAMPLE QUESTIONS:

- In your opinion, what makes this organisation a great place to work?

- What do you consider the most important criteria for success in this job?

- Tell me about the organisation's culture.

- How will my performance be evaluated?

- What are the opportunities for advancement?

- What are the next steps in the hiring process?

Be strategic. Cover information not discussed or clarify a previous topic - do not ask for information that can be found on the organisation's website: it makes you look sloppy and unprepared.

Checklist for interviewing best practice

- Present a fitting image for the part you seek. Walk, talk, and look the part.

- Likeability is vital. Act confident and friendly with good eye contact, a strong handshake, and a lot of smiles. Don't use first names unless asked to do so.

- Memorise a twenty to thirty second branding brief. Your branding brief should tell your story very quickly.

- Master a one to two minute 'commercial' - the elevator pitch. A lot of interviews will begin with an open question, eg 'tell me a little about yourself'. Memorise a short description of your background (education, experience, and skills) that matches your strengths to the job. Add a sentence or two about your curiosity, commitment, and drive to build on your already impressive skills base.

- Don't chatter to fill a silence. You risk nervously blurting out harmful information. Instead, ask a question: 'Would you rather hear about my skills in A or B?'

- Develop a story-telling knack. Prepare short little true stories that support your claims of relevant skills and accomplishments.

10

SOD'S LAW

'If something can go wrong, it will.'
Sod (presumably)

'Success consists of going from failure to failure
without loss of enthusiasm.'
**Sir Winston Churchill or Abraham Lincoln
depending on who you believe**

That's quite a pessimistic interpretation of the law of sod so I prefer to embrace the glass half full version of it which is more along the lines of 'prepare for the worst, hope for the best.' Yes, it is true the best laid plans do not always go the way you imagined and things can blindside you and throw you off course. What's important in these moments is to regroup quickly and get creative.

The Eton Mess - so the story goes, a parent of a pupil at Eton School way back when brought a pavlova - cream, strawberries and meringue to a school picnic to watch a cricket match. The family pet, a black Labrador jumped onto the picnic basket crushing all its contents. Rather than discard it, the enterprising mother simply dubbed it an Eton Mess and so the delicious pudding was born. Yes, it's a jokey example, but it serves to highlight a point: things happen but it doesn't mean that disaster is imminent.

To use another example - a while back the England rugby team had been number one in the world for a number of years. They won the World Cup and then almost overnight they stalled; they had run out of ideas. Now they are flying high again under a new manager. They continue to field a very similar team to the one that crashed out of the World Cup they were hosting in 2015, but with fresh ideas and, importantly, a new rule that the manager has imposed - if a player is tackled he has to be back on his feet in under three seconds. That's what you need to do, get back on your feet as quickly as possible. Don't give in to feelings of upset or failure, just get up and get back in the game. There will be things that happen to you, things you can't control, results that won't go your way, setbacks and failures. They are inevitable and largely unimportant. What is important is how you cope with these, what actions you take to correct your course and get back on the track you set for yourself.

So let's explore some of the things that can go wrong and how it is not just possible but sometimes even advantageous for you to bounce back from them.

Failure, far from not being an option, is an inevitable consequence of trying. If you put yourself out there then things will go wrong, but let's not get hung up on the negative connotations of the word; in fact let's change the word to something altogether friendlier. Let's call it a blip. So, blips happen. In fact as we look back at the examples of many, if not all, of the case studies, blips happen all the time, even to very successful people. The way the interviews were presented would suggest that I was trying to show the differing routes to success across a variety of sectors and yes, all of them are hard-working, industrious and outward-thinking people who have embraced their passions and pursued them doggedly. Some have done things very differently to the manner in which I would suggest is a more logical path to success and some of them have done many of the things that I would describe as best practice. As I mentioned before, there's no one right way but there are lots of wrong ways. But, over-ridingly, each and every one of them has suffered setbacks, blips, that they have gone on to use to their advantage. Sometimes that blip can send them off on a tangent, through which they end up pursuing a path that leads them to greater success than they had previously imagined.

In the example of Wayne Hemingway, it was because of a blip that he ended up founding a fashion empire. He couldn't pay his rent so took the initiative, sold some clothes and that became his business.

OLIVER JONES, THE JUDGE - he failed to get pupillage the first time around so he went and worked for a year, gained more experience, got his masters and got his pupillage the next time. Arguably, doing what he did made him a more complete lawyer and a more compelling prospect to the pupillage committee.

SARAH ANN KENNEDY - became a household name with Peppa Pig after an accident and parenthood changed her plans for the future.

DAVID MOONEY - it was because the family business was failing that he overhauled it and did things differently that led to greater success and being able to buy up further restaurants.

KEITH JOBLING - after finishing university knew he wanted to do something very different to what he'd trained for.

DR. BARRY GIBB - only by recognising that he'd made mistakes with some of the roles he'd taken did he more fully understand himself and adapt his longer term goals to meet his career interests.

ELLIOT RASHMAN - lost his tools on a building site and went on to be a wildly successful music manager.

Some of these blips you may not recognise or characterise as being failures per se, but that's semantics, whatever you choose to call them; certain aspects of their working lives weren't in line with what they wanted and they proactively used that starting point as an impetus to change. Learning from your mistakes is an important part of growing up: identifying where things haven't gone to plan and then figuring out a way to either turn that to your advantage or using it as an opportunity to better understand what you are looking to achieve.

So, if we take a few likely examples of potential blips that you may encounter:

Not getting the grades you expected

This is one that many of you will encounter and there's little you can do about it once it's done. The peculiarity of applying for university, which is probably the single largest reason for why good grades are going to be paramount in your thinking, is that you are applying for courses based on your predicted grades. But anything can happen, good or bad.

THE GOOD VERSION - maybe you applied for certain courses or certain universities based on your predicted grades, you ended up compromising on those choices and now you've got much better grades than expected and find yourself in the unenviable position of taking up a place on a course that you were never in love with. Don't do something you're only lukewarm about: if you wildly over-achieve and that gives you a shot at something you'd love, then don't compromise. You could take your chances in clearing, of course, but another route would be to take the year, organise some really interesting gap year experiences, work a little, get an internship and then reapply for the course or college that you really wanted in the first place. You'll have more to say, you'll have broadened your horizons and you may be better prepared for the challenges that lie ahead at a more competitive university.

THE BAD VERSION - very similar to the good version: not getting the grades needn't be a death sentence on your dream. If you missed the boat, you could take the year, do re-sits, do additional training, gain additional experiences that may bolster applications. You could, as many of my clients have done, opt to take a lesser degree or course with the aim of converting the following year. The important thing is not to panic but rather to take a few deep breaths, recognise what has happened then try and work around the blip.

Grades are not the full story. Yes, universities are perhaps slightly more binary in their approach but for something like an apprenticeship there is maybe more latitude to appeal to their better natures and that is why having a raft of interesting experiences, referees and so on can become so important. By having that robust personal portfolio to draw upon the grades may just carry slightly less weight; everyone has bad days and professors, employers, etc know that too.

Not getting on to the course (university or apprenticeship) you hoped to.

As with the grades, get creative. At university you can go though clearing, you can get to the right university and then transfer when there are inevitably a few drop outs: broadly speaking, for every four places offered only one is taken up. Universities like to pretend that they are massively oversubscribed but that's not the reality. A lot of places cynically offer lots of places to students who will never get the grades because they believe saying there are 200 plus applicants for every place makes them look special. It's all smoke and mirrors. Equally, you could get on a course that is related to what you were hoping to do and then transfer, sometimes between universities, or to a course that is actually what you want to do. Necessity is the mother of invention, so goes the expression, so when you need something, be inventive.

Not getting the job/internship/ apprenticeship you wanted

This is a tough one, and the hardest thing is that it will always feel personal. It will feel like someone has met you, spoken to you, and then made a decision that you are either simply not good enough or that they couldn't bear to work alongside you. Unfortunately sometimes that will be true, *but* most of the time it will be for reasons outside of your control: maybe they met someone who had more direct experience, interviewed better on the day, got on better with the manager from a cultural fit perspective, had aspirations that were more in line with their expectations of the role, placement, internship, etc.

Rather than burn your bridges by sulking and pouting, drop them an email thanking them for the opportunity, express your continued interest and ask whether there was any specific feedback that you could work on for the future. Turn that negative into a potential asset. Consider every blip to be a learning opportunity: you didn't get this one, so what? You'll get the next. What can you learn? What feedback can they offer that will help you refine your pitch, your interview skills and so on? Consider it live practice and move on to the next thing - as we looked at before, when making work experience approaches, you should try and have lots of opportunities on the go at once. By practising and refining your approach, you are learning to be more self-aware and self-critical. This is an opportunity to work on your presentation skills and, by the time you are in front of your dream employer, you'll be ready.

Also, don't be too hard on yourself. Be aware and take the lessons learned; sometimes you just won't have the right set of experiences, or rather someone you were up against had slightly more. It is for precisely this reason that doing all you can to gain interesting and varied experiences is so important and why you should all be doing everything you can. That said though, sometimes it's just not your day. I've been unsuccessful at interviews dozens of times and sure, it always smarts a little, but you take something away from it.

An example of this is when I worked at the BBC my contract was coming to an end and I went for an interview with ITV to work on *Kids Stars in their Eyes*. The interview went fine; it was all going great guns and then, just as it was wrapping up and I was on my way out of the door, they asked if I watched the show and I said, 'No, to be honest I find it morally repugnant' - not, as I should have said, 'All the time. I love it'. Not even, 'not really, but when I have, I do enjoy it.' Needless to say, I learned a little something that day and I didn't even have to ask for feedback.

Making the wrong decision

Sometimes you will find that somewhere along the line you have made a terrible error of judgement. Now if you're lucky you pick up on it quickly and you can make a few changes and you're back on course. Other times it takes longer to realise and consequently the decision to make changes seems much bigger.

FOR EXAMPLE - let's say you always wanted to be a doctor. You choose your GCSEs and A levels based on that premise and aggressively pursue work experience etc designed to impress an admissions board. Towards the time when it comes to applying for university you begin to second-guess your choice and start to think that actually you're much more interested in becoming a financial advisor. 'Well,' you may think, 'I've done so much in support of that first goal that it seems like a waste to change at this stage. I'd be throwing away all that effort.' Now, if you stack the effort of a couple of years against the idea of throwing away your life in a career you're no longer interested in, then it seems like a safe bet to go for the new option, but because of our natural loss aversion you will be sorely tempted to ignore your gut. Don't. Instead you can re-frame your experiences and in your application make the point that for a long time you thought your career was going to be medicine but as you've got older you became increasingly interested in pursuing a career in financial advising and then focus on the transferable skills, intellectual capacity, eye for detail, statistical analysis and interpretation and so on. Don't be afraid to reassess; it's not a sign of weakness or dithering if done correctly, but a recognition of what you want and a proactive decision not to go too far down a path that you no longer want to be on. Don't be too proud to admit when you've made a mistake.

The temptation upon recognising that you may've embarked upon the wrong path is to be terribly British about it and just stick at it. Sometimes that makes sense but, as we covered before, at this time in your life compromising and going with the flow may not serve you as well longer term. If you've picked the wrong A levels, the sooner you recognise that the better. It's not too late to make changes. Don't keep quiet and hope it'll get better.

If you've picked the wrong career goal, by doing work experience, informational interviewing and so on, hopefully you will have negated the possibility of this happening to a pretty fine degree, but sometimes you will change your mind as you grow older and learn more about what you want from life. Don't compound the wrong decision by just putting your head down; you'll be wasting your time. Think about a constructive route out of it, make sensible decisions regarding what training, course, subjects, you need to study to access that new goal.

In short, you will stumble, you are fallible and mistakes will be made. Don't try and avoid them, simply be aware that they will happen, prepare for different eventualities, have back-up plans, have back-up plans for your back-up plans. If you're lucky you'll never have to use them. Indeed the whole point of this book is to do all the little things well enough that the big stuff slots into place but should the blip, blip then don't panic, embrace the new opportunity and use it as a chance to learn something new or different or interesting that can help further your understanding or get you closer to where you are supposed to be.

CASE STUDY
ELLIOT RASHMAN

One of the most successful British band managers of the last thirty years, managing Simply Red, James and The Happy Mondays, formerly a joiner, Entertainments Manager at UMIST and now a writer, mentor, Marxist, polymath and aging hippie.

ME: To kick things off can you just give me a potted history of you and your career, educational background, etc?

ER: I went for six years to North Manchester Grammar until the age of sixteen and hated every second of it and it gave me very little. I then went to Salford Tech to do my A levels. I was streamed at the age of fourteen into the sciences which I failed at A level abysmally because the streaming processes in this country are based on a paucity of information about the pupils and assumptions are made far too early. Then I did three A levels in one year in an intensive course at Salford Tech, having failed Biology, Physics and Chemistry A level, and I sailed through them. I did English, Sociology and History and that's because I was badly streamed originally. I then went on to what's now called Manchester Met but was Manchester Polytechnic back then. I did humanities and I specialised in English and American Literature and Socio-Economic History and Political Institutions and I got a 2:1.

It was the kind of degree where there was no practical career at the end of it unless you were their one person that they had an MA for or you were going to be teacher. At that point very little happened work-wise, to the point where after about two or three years of floundering I went and did a two year apprenticeship, an intense apprenticeship in joinery, which was partly to prove to myself that I could use my hands as well as the bullsh*t in my brain. I then went and became a joiner for Halifax council for two years. Then I worked for myself for a couple of years and all through my time from the age of sixteen I worked with musical friends, and I was the non-musician who would help out. It was pre roadie-ing, roadie-ing and support and the opportunity to apply. Well, what actually happened is my tools got stranded during a horrendous winter in Yorkshire on a job and I found myself unemployed and applied for a job in the *Guardian* to be an Entertainments Manager at UMIST and I got the job. Within a year I was poached by Manchester Polytechnic's Student Union to be their Entertainments Manager in a brand new facility.

ME: How old was this then, about thirty?

ER: A bit younger, about twenty-eight. Before that I also did a year on work experience at Granada on a programme called *Reports Action* which was a live programme that went out on a Sunday which was a social community programme. It was originally fronted by Anna Ford and then by Dame Joan Bakewell.

ME: How did that come about? Was that through doing the Entertainments stuff?

ER: No, it was before then - it was just something I did that came about through a friend. It was half Granada and half CVS which was a voluntary services group, a large voluntary services group, and it was about community. It went out live on a Sunday and it was about things like - for example, they had a stop smoking campaign where they sent out stop smoking kits and five million people applied for it. I worked on something that was quite innovative at the time. It was a kind of warning signal that attached to bicycles to prevent cyclists being knocked over and about two million people applied for that and it had a live phone-in element and then you researched different angles and different appeals and then I went off and became an Entertainment Manager and that was probably only the second Entertainment Manager in the country at the time. Student Unions had become commercial entities because they had bars and bars took in money and in order to keep the bars full of students you needed entertainment and post Punk a lot of the student union's Social Secretaries lost loads of money so student unions decided to make it a managerial position. I did that at UMIST for a year then Manchester Poly for nearly five years and it was through my time at UMIST that I met [Mick] Hucknall who was singing in a band but was also a DJ that I employed. I eventually went on to manage him and put together and name the group around him which was *Simply Red*. I then worked in the music industry for twenty years, more than twenty years. I did Mick Hucknall from '82 to '96. I then deliberately left, as I quit the music industry for a while and then went back and I managed *James*, Ian McCulloch [*Echo & The Bunnymen*] and eventually *The Happy Mondays* and then I quit again.

ME: Why did you quit?

ER: I quit because I had got to the top, and I did, I was responsible for helping to sell forty million albums and I hated the people at the top of the music business itself. I found it to be very self-serving, narcissistic, very mercenary. I went into it because I had an obsession with, and I still do, with the art of music and that's why I did it. But the music business is about business and whilst I was accidently very good at it in terms of business, for example in the case of *Simply Red* from the minute he signed I managed to negotiate quite breath-taking deals on his behalf and they were deals that were relatively unprecedented at that point. It wasn't a part that I particularly enjoyed though. I could do it and I could do it well but it didn't mean anything. It was partly about money and I was Marxist; I still am and I believe in the State not in individuals, because individuals left to their own devices are usually greedy and not really interested in the wellbeing or welfare of the greater good. I was born in 1952. I was a baby-boomer old hippie and that was at odds with the music business. It wasn't really interested in how good the music was, it was interested in how many units it sold and it stopped an interest in originality and I was interested in the art, and I'm still interested in all art forms and that's my main love in life.

ME: So what brought you back?

ER: Um, Tony Wilson - he asked me to manage *The Happy Mondays* because Shaun Ryder was about to go to jail and he asked me to help him out and I did. I also found that once most musicians

reached fame and wealth, they actually became
the things they despised. They lost what gave
them the rebelliousness that made their art work.
Eventually they just become comfortable and safe
and couched. There's very little restlessness.
Once the fame hits, their talent dries up, because
it's very hard to write in an original way when
all you're seeing the world from is rose-tinted,
cushioned glasses from a limo, five star hotels and
restaurants. The pop industry particularly tends to
spoil its children.

ME: What did you do after your second stint in the
industry?

ER: I started to do teaching and mentoring and one
of the things I did was create and co-found
what became known as the Music Management
Forum which is a worldwide organisation, set up
originally to lobby on behalf of managers and
artists to get better deals in the music business.
Because the music business, the thing that
enflamed me was how onerous and exploitative the
deals were for artists.

ME: Already by this point you had had three quite
distinct and very different careers. Was any of
this the result of a plan?

ER: No. If I'm honest, no. The music part of it was the
result of my dream to work with music.

ME: What gave you and those you dealt with the
confidence to believe that you could manage a
band based on your prior experience? Did you
have any expectations that they and you would be
so successful?

ER: No, you don't know where it's going to. What you have to have is a belief in yourself and in this case, the art and the artist and in my case that belief was militant and unwavering and the rest is, what I like to tell people, the rest of music management is the same as any other management. It's an MBA, and ultimately it's about getting the best people, it's understanding the language of all the various aspects, but ultimately it's about representing your artists as strongly as humanly possible.

ME: How do you feel when you look back on your career and how you ordered it, the gambles you took and so on?

ER: I look at it that I got into it because of my love of music and I got out of it because of my love of music. In order to preserve it. I was lucky because people were interested in Hucknall's voice, not his song writing, not the band we put together and not me. I just fought my corner but the rest of it, the rest of my career, was making a list of common sense intuitive decisions as they arise. I think that you can sit down and plot away but it's like John Lennon said, 'Life is what happens to you when you're busy doing other things'.

ME: [Laughs]. I've even quoted that at the beginning of one of the chapters.

ER: It's one of the few things that John Lennon said that was actually salient. I agree with that a great deal, in that when I started to go out there and mentor and I didn't do what people expected me to do. They expected me to come in and talk about a career path, and what I would always say to those people was, you've got this career path and then your partner gets cancer, you have to make decisions - your career path is meaningless at that point. Your strength of character and your growth as a human being will be the things that matter. Because life is one big curveball. I've met so many people that were great in their positions but were made redundant through no fault of their own and it's being able to roll with those punches. A career plan is basically a wish list. It's about the process of knowing thyself. If it's good enough for Hamlet...

ME: So having a wish list is good but you have to be flexible and adapt to change?

ER: There is no way of knowing up front everything you'll ever need to know to get to where you want to be going so the more that you can - my Dad, who was quite a simple man, had one thing he'd always say: in a storm always tie yourself to bamboo, not to a tree, because bamboo bends with the wind. Just look at how the world has changed irrevocably in the last twelve months (Brexit, Trump coming to power, and so on.) The odds are stacked against you. If you're from a poor estate and go to a sh*t secondary school, even if you work hard and are conscientious you are swimming against the tide, and you can't rely on anyone else so you have to box clever.

ME: That's why I hope a book like this could be important because this is something schools aren't doing well.

ER: I absolutely agree. To borrow a Frank Zappa aphorism, he used to say, 'go to the libraries and educate yourselves, don't rely on the schools, don't rely on anybody else' - because all that information is available at your finger tips and now even more so. It's down to personal conscientiousness to want to learn and to never stop learning.

ME: But sometimes it's less to do with the capacity to learn but more that the ambition to do so isn't fostered.

ER: If you're in a home with no magazines, no books, no art, no literature, where thinking and speaking isn't encouraged, then you're going to struggle.

ME: So to you how important is it to shrug off that parental or societal conditioning in order to break away and pursue what you want?

ER: They have to swim against the tide - that's the natural state of affairs.

ME: So what's your advice or recommendation for someone facing those kinds of challenges?

ER: To be educationally pugilistic. To fight. To not be put off if you're a slow learner. Don't be put off if the information doesn't go in instantly. Don't be put off if you struggle to overcome the subject matter that you're looking at. You can persevere, look for encouragers. Always ask questions. It's unfashionable advice now, careers advice, and I've seen this recently on a mentor programme is that they're told to 'shut the fu*k up' and do what they're told. That's what happens in a zero hours market place, where they've no more than three minutes to urinate. Hang on to your enlightenment in an unenlightened market; it's going to be a hostile environment. You have to grow a thick skin. Always be yourself and make yourself of value. Be prepared to learn but don't be put off 'cause it will be hard. It is hard not to be discouraged. The first week at the gym is different to the first week of the second year at the gym. I'm sixty-five now and I have no value so what I would say to young people is to help change society so that when you're my age you live in a society where you still have a value. So do what you can to make the kind of life you want for yourself, but profoundly understand that all that can change tomorrow. If you're only happy in your career and that disappears then you've nothing left. Always look to be outside of your comfort zone and push yourself.

ME: Thank you.

11

BE HERE NOW

'If the whole world depends on the youth of today, I can't see the world lasting another 100 years.'

Socrates

'The youth of today are the leaders of tomorrow.'

Nelson Mandela

So Socrates was majestically wrong when it came to his withering assessment of youth. Evidently even two and a half thousand years ago each generation despaired of the one nipping at its heels. Nelson Mandela had a slightly kinder and more optimistic outlook. You are the leaders of tomorrow, you stand as the vanguard of the future, but before you get there you have to toughen up and get some perspective.

Unfortunately you, my young charges, have been born into a world where from a very early age you have been coddled and cosseted by school, society and your parents. Everyone's a winner; no one can lose. Participation is all. 'You came last? No problem, have a medal.' 'Well done, you were tenth runner up'. I see it at my kids' school at sports day. No one gets called out for cheating, no one wins, no one loses - everything is equal. Yes there's something to be said for protecting kids from the harshness of losing and making them feel bad, but surely it's better you learn now rather than at twenty-five. It's just delaying the inevitable.

Why am I telling you this? Because unfortunately you have come up through that system and increasingly employers are having to pick up the slack and give young entry level workers a crash course in how life actually works. When we talk about the skills that are lacking in industry and that employers are actively seeking, the temptation is to think we only mean actual, practical skills like being a mechanic or knowing how to do spreadsheets (all of which are also true), but what they are really missing is a bunch of people who are prepared to take responsibility for their actions.

When you are brought up through a system that is so forgiving that even the language has been changed to soft-soap success or failure into phrases like 'not meeting expectation' then it's hardly surprising that you are ill-prepared for that first knockback. You can pretty much get to the end of school in an almost consequence-free environment where nothing you do really matters: your parents can barter grades for you, you can change sets to better suit your abilities, and as long as you are really, really trying, everyone is very understanding. But at the point when it starts to matter, your A level results, your BTEC results, etc then almost from left field - BOOM - pass or fail, do not pass go, move directly to jail. How did this happen? Your plan, your goals and ambitions hang on certain results and then after eighteen years of nothing really mattering, suddenly it matters and you are expected to adapt and accept that almost overnight. Others can get all the way through university and into their first jobs before they find themselves in the shallow end of the pool with no trunks - an employer asks for an idea and they don't have the right answer; suddenly results matter. That kind of binary approach between schooling and real life leads to people hating their jobs, changing their jobs, regretting their decisions and questioning their whole plan.

So again, why am I telling you this? We talked before about the importance of staying the course, about not letting little things distract and rattle you, about the greener grass brainworm phenomenon and this is kind of the same thing. When things go wrong, and they will, no matter what job you are doing, the temptation is to blame your boss for being hard or mean, or blame the decision process that led to you being there - basically anything other than having to look at the part you played in that process. Looking over that metaphorical fence to see what's on the other side, thinking about moving on to the next thing, because this thing just 'isn't you', blaming others, blaming poor decisions are all just defence mechanisms designed to remove the finger of doubt away from you. Life can be harsh and there are days when it will kick your arse. You need to prepare for that and, more importantly, you need to learn from that. The best people I've ever known both professionally and personally are those who have chosen to embrace personal accountability and when something challenges them, rather than turn tail or break down and cry, they rise to the challenge, accept the part they've played in it and look to how they could do things differently.

I was stupid enough to get married very young and inevitably divorced not much later. - For a long time I blamed my ex-wife, although in fairness she did go on to a have a child remarkably soon with a co-worker so I think some of my suspicions weren't without merit. After a while though I began to consider what I might have done differently; what could I learn from that process? As hard and as difficult as it was, I had to consider the possibility that there is perhaps more I could and should have done. Looking back, not getting married so young in the first place was probably the better idea but through that process I hope and believe that I grew and learned some things about myself that I have continued to use as I've grown older. Jobs, like relationships, in every sense including friendships, colleagues and so on, require constant work and reassessment of what your goals are, where you want to be, how you communicate, how you respond to criticism, what you could do better or differently.

If you want to have a career that fulfils you and one where you can have an impact, then you need to develop a tougher skin than the one you've likely been walking around in up until now. Even the toughest, roughest people you know, who may argue that their life is already hard and their parents hate them and beat them and they grew up through the care system or whatever it might be, are frail and sensitive. Yes, I know how that sounds and I'm no way trying to be reductive about anyone's experiences, no matter how privileged or tough, but the reality is to look inside yourself and accept criticism is not the same thing as being able to take a beating or be called names all day long - that's not about you, that's about them. To look inside yourself and truly consider who you want to be and how you can work towards that goal is going to mean having to process criticism in a productive way. The sting of criticism is real but true things are painful; it's what you do with that pain that defines your future, not the criticism itself.

The title of the chapter, as well as being the second-worst of Oasis' albums, is about being present in your life. Not to be an observer cynically commenting on why things went wrong, but to allow yourself to feel, to understand what happened, good or bad, and then using that information to develop, grow and learn.

For all the many great things that social media has to offer, it may also be the worst thing that happened to your generation. Instagram, Facebook, mobile phones et al, all add to the promotion of instant gratification, which serves only to take you out of the present. When you can preen, tweak and filter every aspect of your life to be captured forever on the internet and see others doing the same, it removes any need to interact and learn anything meaningful,: a 'like' or a 'thumbs-up' has begun to define our worth. Hiding behind keyboards, bragging about superficially glamorous lives, is not just a waste of time but it actively undermines your confidence and leads to feelings of isolation and depression. People having actual enjoyment don't feel the need to stop everything to photograph and geo-tag it.

It's so easy to see all that stuff and think it's real but it's just another way for the world to chip away at your confidence and contribute to the feelings of inadequacy that you will be dealing with when you don't get that job, get told no, get told you've failed, that your idea sucks, and so on, and everyone else is leading rich, thrilling lives. Collectively everyone you ever met is having the BEST TIME EVER and no one even 'liked' a picture of your dog. How can life be so cruel?

If everyone is having the best time ever - and you'll know they are because they hashtagged it - your own life will inevitably seem pretty sucky by comparison, which in turn can make you question your life decisions, your choices, your job, which brings us back to the beginning. Stay the course - Rome wasn't built in a day - and when you spend your life and time defining yourself by 'thumbs-up's and laughing tears emojis, you become very used to instantaneous praise and feedback and your expectation is that life should be like that too. Life isn't like that, jobs aren't like that and even the most ambitious people can end up being a valued, but essentially replaceable, part of a business and even then it takes a long time to get there. Whilst greatness may exist in all of you, being good at your job and happy in your life is more than many can even hope for, but when you see social media it can make you feel like anything less than perfect is a failure: it's not. It's realistic.

So when you take that first knock-back, see it for what it is - a stepping stone, a learning experience. You may have really wanted whatever that thing was but life isn't like that; you don't get that same instant success or affirmation that you can find online and for many of us that's enough to make us question everything rather than take it on the chin and keep trying.

If I were to tell you the jobs I had before I ended up here, sitting at my desk typing these words, you might begin to understand how twisty turny these things can be. Sometimes you have to go the long way round and because I went a *really* long way round I can hopefully help you to find some of those shortcuts. For me and many I know, success didn't happen overnight - hell, I'm still searching for it now - it was long, laborious and hard, but I didn't grow up thinking it was going to be any different.

So to conclude, don't define yourself by how many 'thumbs-up' you get; don't expect everything to happen straight away - anything worth having is worth working and waiting for; don't take every criticism or failure personally - it's an opportunity for learning and growth; and occasionally look up from your phones to embrace the world around you. You may just learn something new that you can't find online.

CONCLUSION

'Life's like a movie, write your own ending.
Keep believing, keep pretending.'

Jim Henson

The guy who said the above invented Kermit and Miss Piggy, so, you know...

In spite of the potentially headline-grabbing title, 'Is your School Lying to You?' hopefully what you'll take away from this is not that I'm against schools or that I'm all about trying to point fingers. Your school does, I'm quite certain, want the very best for you. But they lack the foresight, the resources and the expertise. Often victims of their own hubris, they unfortunately are political silly putty having to constantly bend and manipulate themselves to meet the latest set of arbitrary targets laid down by the government. This should in no way concern you. What the government wants for you is far less important than what you want for yourself.

Think about that for a moment - what you want for yourself. No matter who you are, where you've started from, what your parents did or didn't do, no matter your colour, your religion, your sexuality, your gender, if you want something from your life don't let others tell you 'No'. They don't define your worth, you do. To paraphrase Martin Luther King Jr., 'be judged by the content of your character'. If you have a desire, a dream or an ambition, the only one holding you back is you. Yes, many of you will have steeper hills to climb but that will just make your success so much sweeter. There is nothing, no excuse that you can offer, that can excuse a squandered life. You only get one go around (unless you're into reincarnation) so make it spectacular.

So when your school tries to push you towards a degree or a university that isn't what you want or when they try to discourage you from pursuing a certain path because it's 'not for the likes of you', nod your head and do what you want. It's your life, not theirs, and over the last few years they've got a really, really bad reputation when it comes to getting this stuff right. Not only are they not the experts, there is sadly a sort of widespread fiefdom-building mentality that means the shutters go down when people like me approach them and offer to help, sometimes free of charge, and they just deny there's a problem and that they are doing it all anyway, and yah boo. Anyone who thinks they know everything and doesn't need any help is not someone I'd trust, and you shouldn't either.

When it comes to your future, accept the help that's on offer but seek out corroborating evidence, see what other people and places recommend, be the captain of your own ship and don't be afraid to sail into the storm. Yes, there may be hiccups and things may not always be easy, but I sincerely believe that by taking a pro-active stance and following the steps laid out in this book you give yourself a much greater chance of success than listening to people whose limitations are inevitable, given the jobs they do.

So in conclusion, be prepared to work hard, set goals, put yourself out there, don't just do the bare minimum to box tick, recognise that every piece of homework you do is not to get the teacher off your back but has a direct and clear link to whatever your future might be. Every choice you make has a consequence and every setback is an opportunity to learn. The power to make your life everything you've ever wanted is within you. If you ever need to be reminded of that, read 'Oh, the places you'll go!' by Dr. Seuss.

Carpe the hell out of that diem and good luck, I know you'll be extraordinary!

BIBLIOGRAPHY

Robert Louis Stephenson - *Virginibus Puerisque* (1881).

Allen Saunders - *Reader's Digest/Publishers Syndicate* (January 1957).

Daniel Kahneman - *Thinking Fast and Slow* (Penguin 2012).

Earl Nightingale - *Lead the Field* (BN Publishing 2007).

Aldous Huxley - *The Perennial Philosophy* (Harper & Brothers 1945).

Professor Daniel Wilson - *Prehistoric Man: Researches into the Origin of Civilisation in the Old and the New World* (MacMillan & Co. 1862).

Daniel Goleman - *Social Intelligence: The New Science of Human Relationships* (Arrow 2007).

Daniel Goleman - *Emotional Intelligence & Working with Emotional Intelligence* (Bloomsbury Publishing Plc. 2004).

Chip Conley - *Public Domain (but reproduced with kind permission)*.

Janine Willis & Alexander Todorov - *First Impressions* (Psychological Science July 2006).

Dr. Seuss - *Oh, the places you'll go!* (Harper Collins Children's Publishing 2006).

ACKNOWLEDGEMENTS

Firstly I would like to thank my wife Dina, without her warmth and constancy I wouldn't be inspired to do a thing, my children, Oscar, Ralph & Mia who gave me a reason to start caring about education again and my family who have been so supportive during the whole process, reading, sense checking and critiquing my efforts and endlessly reposting all the blogs, pictures and tiresome social media cavalcade.

I would of course like to thank all the contributors who gave so willingly of their time and agreed to share their experiences with me, so a big thank you to Oliver Jones, Barry Gibb, Elliot Rashman, David Mooney, Keith Jobling, Sarah Ann Kennedy and Wayne Hemingway.

I would like to thank Dr. Ruairidh Macleod for all his help on the science, academic side of things and pedagogy, Ian Ronson for helping galvanise my approach to careers planning and Jenny Rutter for helping me reach out to the contributors.

Finally I'd like to thank Alice Solomons of FAB Publishing for offering me the opportunity to write this book and have it find an audience. I believe in the importance of what it teaches and after years of the simple message being ignored by schools and the media it was incredibly heartening to meet someone who shared the view that we can do better by our children.